PREPARING TO BE CONFIRMED

A programme of preparation for
the sacrament of confirmation

Diana Klein

McCrimmons
Great Wakering, Essex, England

First published in 2002 in United Kingdom by
McCRIMMON PUBLISHING CO. LTD.,
10-12 High Street, Great Wakering, Essex, SS3 0EQ
Email: info@mccrimmons.com
sales@mccrimmons.com
Website: www.mccrimmons.com

ISBN 085597 643 8

Nihil obstat - Fr. Anton Cowan, Censor

Imprimatur - The Very Rev. Alan Hopes, Vicar General
Westminster, August 15, 2002,
The Feast of the Assumption of the Blessed Virgin Mary

The Nihil obstat and Imprimatur are a declaration that a book or pamphlet is considered to be free from doctrinal or moral error. It is not implied that those who have granted the Nihil obstat and Imprimatur agree with the contents, opinions or statements expressed.

Acknowledgements

Scripture texts used in this work are taken from the *New Revised Standard Version Bible: Catholic Edition*, copyright © 1993 and 1989 by the National Council of the Churches of Christ in the USA. Used with permission. All rights reserved.

References have been made to the:

General Directory for Catechesis, copyright © 1997, Congregation for the Clergy, Catholic Truth Society, publishers to the Holy See, London.

Dei Verbum, Lumen Gentium and *Sacrosanctum Concilium* taken from *Vatican Council II and Post Conciliar Documents* edited by Austin Flannery, OP copyright © 1975, 1986, 1992, 1996, Costello Publishing Company, Inc., Northport, NY.

Catechesi Tradendae, Pope John Paul II to the Episcopate, the Clergy and the Faithful of the Entire Church on Catechesis in our Time, 1979.

The Catechism of the Catholic Church, Geoffrey Chapman, London, 1994.

The Rite of Christian Initiation of Adults, Office of the Sacred Congregation for Divine Worship, copyright © February 19, 1987 and the Rite of Confirmation, © August 22, 1971.

The Code of Canon Law, Collins Liturgical Publications, London, copyright © 1983.

Africa: Our Way to be God's Messengers, A Handbook for Catechists and Pastoral Workers, Sr. Nicole Grégoire, S.A. and Michael McGrath, S.M.A., Redwood Books, Trowbridge, Wiltshire, copyright © 1990.

Excerpts have been used with permission and all rights are reserved from:

Oh God, Why? By Gerard W. Hughes, The Bible Reading Fellowship, Oxford, copyright © 1993.

The Eucharist, Raymond Topley, Maynooth, copyright © 1990.

Christian Religious Education, Sharing the Vision, by Tom Groome, published by Harper Collins Publishers, New York, copyright © 1980.

Christ the Encounter with God, Edward Schillebeeckx, Sheed & Ward, London, © 1966. Sheed & Ward is an imprint of The Rowman & Littlefield Publishing Group, Lanham, Inc.

Design and layout: Nick Snode
Cover illustration: The Benedictine Sisters Turvey Abbey
Ten Commandments illustration: Nicholas J. Klein
Typeset in Verdana 11/14 and ITC Eras
Printed & bound by www.printondemand-worlwide.com, UK

A/AF

Contents

Foreword

I am delighted to have been invited to write a foreword for *Preparing to be Confirmed*. I observed this programme growing and developing over the years while I was an Auxiliary Bishop in Westminster – particularly when Diana Klein was working with me as Area Catechist in West London.

The Sacrament of Confirmation confirms and strengthens what happens in Baptism – when we are marked for Christ, when we are called to become like Him and to do His work. Most of our teenagers were baptised as infants; it was their parents and godparents who spoke on their behalf. How important it is for our young people to be prepared well to celebrate the Sacrament of Confirmation – so that they can declare for themselves what they believe.

Preparing to be Confirmed is based on Scripture and draws on the life experiences of the candidates – linking the two and helping the young people to deepen their relationship with Christ through conversation and prayer. It challenges them to think about being followers of Christ – and the difference that makes in the choices in their lives.
The programme provides the kind of easy, practical and prayerful guidance that catechists need for their work and it appeals to the young people. I hope you will find it helpful.

† Patrick O'Donoghue
Bishop of Lancaster

Introduction

A note to the catechists about Preparing for Confirmation

This programme has been written after more than ten years of experience preparing young people for the sacrament of confirmation and after many years helping catechists to know how to prepare the young people. It reflects the experience, ideas and advice of the priests and the many catechists and candidates I have worked with.

In the winter of 1991, my parish priest approached me; he wondered if I would be willing to help with confirmation preparation in the parish. My son was about 14 years old at the time; this made me something of an expert with youngsters of that age, he thought. I very reluctantly agreed to help – but only to help. Like many new catechists, I did not think I could do much.

At that time, we could not find a programme we felt we could follow; so, we put together our own programme – as so many people do. Our programme was designed to help the teenagers decide for themselves whether or not they wanted to continue to be Christians. We did not assume that, simply because they agreed to follow the course, they would automatically be confirmed.

We said that the parents of our teenagers have brought them this far on their faith journey; the programme should help them to decide for themselves if they want to continue on this journey. It should help them to decide if they want God to be a part of their lives, whether they want to follow Jesus Christ and whether they are willing to be open to the Holy Spirit.[1]

As it has developed, the programme follows the basic thinking behind the RCIA process.[2] It begins with a short period of enquiry – when the candidates ask what the programme is all about. If they decide they want to prepare to be confirmed, they are introduced to the parish community at a Mass of Enrolment when they ask for their support and prayers. They continue the programme with a period of catechesis, which ends with a Mass of Commitment – when they say they want to continue their preparation. They say they understand the importance of what they are doing and they pray for a deeper growth in faith, hope and love. The last period is one of prayerful preparation; and this culminates in the celebration of the sacrament.

This is the end of the programme of preparation for confirmation; now the post-confirmation period begins and the newly confirmed young people face the prospect of living the Christian life day by day. About a month after the confirmation, meet with the young people offering them the chance to reflect on what they have learned and what they have experienced – remind them how important they are to the community.

---

1 *Catechesi Tradendae*, Pope John Paul II to the Episcopate, the Clergy and the Faithful of the Entire Catholic Church on Catechesis in our Time, 1979, ¶5. Pope John Paul II stressed that at the heart of catechesis, we find, in essence a person, the person of Jesus… who is the way the truth, and the life. He went on to say that to catechise aims to put us in touch, in communion, with Jesus for only he can lead us to the love of the Father in the Spirit.

2 *The Rite of Christian Initiation of Adults*, Office of the Sacred Congregation for Divine Worship, February 19, 1987.

I hope that the notes on the following pages will help you to understand how to use this programme. I am happy to share what I have learned with you.

What is the Confirmation catechist doing?

Over and over again, in the many stories Jesus told and in the way he treated people, he told us what God is like. The apostles were the first catechists; they proclaimed the Good News as they heard it from Jesus. Indeed, the word 'catechesis' means echoing God's word.[3] The apostles went out and proclaimed Jesus in order to lead others to faith in him. From the beginning, they talked about how they burned with the desire to proclaim Christ. They said they could not but speak of what they had seen and heard.[4] And you, as a catechist, are invited to proclaim Christ too.

How do we proclaim Christ to a group of teenagers? We have learned that the nature of God's revelation is much broader than a set of propositions;[5] it is more a question of who is revealed rather than what is revealed.

Let's look at Jesus as the model catechist [6]

On the first Easter Sunday, two of Jesus's followers were making their way to Emmaus, a small village about seven miles from Jerusalem. As they went their way, they discussed "all that had happened" (14) over the previous days, and, as might be expected, it was a "lively exchange" (15). Who should join them but the risen Jesus, who began "to walk along with them" (15). For whatever reason, they were "restrained from recognising him" (16). He entered into their company by inquiring, "What are you discussing along your way?" (17). Somewhat distressed and a little impatient at the stranger's ignorance, they wondered where he had been. Surely, everyone in Jerusalem knew "the things that went on there during these past few days?" (18). Rather than seizing this obvious opportunity to disclose his identity (who knew better than he what had gone on there?), he inquired, "What things?" (19). They told him the story as they knew it and their dwindling hope that "he was the one who would set Israel free" (21). Now, adding confusion to their disappointment, "some women" (22) of the group were spreading the "astonishing news" (22) that "he was alive" (23).

Jesus cajoled them for not looking at these recent events within a broader context, and in response to their story and hope, he told them an older story and a larger vision. "Beginning then, with Moses and all the prophets, he interpreted for them every passage of Scripture, which referred to him" (27). He pointed out that the Messiah had to "undergo all this so as to enter into his glory" (26). Surely now they would recognise him. They did not, and he continued to resist telling them. But he had obviously aroused their curiosity, for they "pressed him" (29) to stay the night in their company. He agreed.

At table that evening, he blessed and broke bread for them and "with that their eyes were opened and they recognised him; whereupon he vanished from their sight" (31).

---

3 It comes from the Greek words *kata* meaning 'down' and *echein* meaning 'to sound'. We translate it as resounding or echoing.

4 Acts 4:20; *Catechism of the Catholic Church* ¶425.

5 *Vatican II, Dei Verbum, Decree on Divine Revelation*, November 18, 1965.

6 Luke 24:13-35. Note: the numbers in brackets refer to the verse number of the Scripture.

Then the pieces of their puzzle fell in place, and they remembered how their hearts had "burned" inside them as he talked "on the road". But instead of spending time in self-reproach for not seeing sooner, they set out immediately for Jerusalem (a hazardous journey by night) to tell "the Eleven and the rest of the company" (33). They told the story of what had happened "on the road" and "how they had come to know him in the breaking of the bread" (35).[7]

The method we use – or the approach we take

What Jesus did with the disciples has inspired the catechetical method or process we use. It is sometimes called the 'pastoral cycle' or the 'shared praxis method'. Tom Groome avoids calling shared praxis a theory or a method because he wants it to be both. He tries to avoid the traditional dichotomy between theory and practice and wants to capture what he calls the twin moments of praxis (reflection and action). Groome prefers to call it an 'approach' – in other words, an informed reflective (theory) manner of doing (method) Christian education.[8]

Sr Nicole Grégoire calls it 'the life approach: 3-step method'[9] and she uses these words to describe it:

> life as we know it —> God's message—> new life or message for my life

Is this not what happened to the disciples when they met Jesus on the road to Emmaus? They talked to Jesus – out of their lived experience – about what had been happening and Jesus listened to them. He broke open the scriptures to help them to understand what had happened. They still did not realise it was Jesus; but he didn't give up. They finally recognised him only when he blessed and broke the bread. They got the message. We use the same method Jesus did – and each session during this preparation programme helps the young people:

- to talk about their life experiences – things that happen in their daily life
- to listen to Scripture (or Tradition) and get help to understand it
- to get a message for their lives, to help them understand how they are to live according to what God has said.

The Church gives us guidelines about what to include in the programme

Confirmation preparation should help us come to know Jesus more deeply

The Catechism tells us that the preparation for confirmation should aim at leading the Christian towards a more intimate union with Christ.[10]

One of the ways we encounter Jesus is in the sacraments; this is somewhere we get an opportunity to know him better – where we are led to a more intimate union with him. You might explain this encounter by talking about what a human glance – a human

7 Paraphrased by Tom Groome, *Christian Religious Education, Sharing the Vision*, Harper Collins Publishers, New York, 1980, pp135-136.

8 Groome, *Christian Religious Education*, p.137.

9 *Africa: Our Way to be God's Messengers, A Handbook for Catechists and Pastoral Workers*, Sr. Nicole Grégoire, SA and Michael McGrath, SMA, Redwood Books, Trowbridge, Wiltshire, 1990, p.151.

10 *Catechism of the Catholic Church (The Catechism)*, Geoffrey Chapman, London, 1994, ¶1309.

smile – can do to us, how by a smile, we can seem to be turned into a new person. In the strength of the love which comes to us in that glance or that smile, everything can change. Edward Schillebeeckx suggests that we should try to conceive how the smile of Jesus – God's smile, the God-man's glance at us – can change our whole life. This, he says, is what the sacraments are: the God-man's expression of love – which we get with all the consequences that go along with it.[11]

Our programme includes a session on the sacraments to help the young people know how they encounter God in Jesus – and how encounters with Jesus did not just take place in history, they continue to take place in our world today.

There is a link between baptism and confirmation

The Introduction to the Rite of Confirmation tells us that confirmation strengthens and confirms what happens in baptism – completing the grace of baptism. This is why the renewal of baptismal promises takes place preceding the reception of the sacrament of confirmation.[12]

Our programme includes a session on the Creed. Studying the Creed, reflecting on it and thinking about it will help to prepare the young people to make this statement of faith – making their own what others proclaimed for them when they were baptised.

The Rite of Confirmation also expresses the link between baptism and confirmation by telling us that it is desirable that the godparent at baptism, if available, should be the sponsor at confirmation. (This does not mean to say they exclude the option of choosing a special sponsor.)[13]

Witnessing or Apostolic Work

Confirmation further initiates our journey of faith. The candidates are admitted to the community with a goal, so they are empowered for that and they are sent to proclaim the good news. The Catechism tells us that the time of preparation for confirmation should help the young people to be more capable of assuming the apostolic responsibilities of Christian life.[14]

Nearly all programmes of preparation for confirmation include a session on the gifts of the Holy Spirit. In our programme, this session helps the young people to see how we can identify these gifts in ourselves and use them for some kind of community project during the preparation period – and, hopefully, ongoing into the future.[15]

---

11 Edward Schillebeeckx, *Christ the Encounter with God*, Sheed & Ward, London, © 1966, pp.78-79.

12 *The Rite of Confirmation*, Sacred Congregation for Divine Worship, Guidelines in the Preface.

13 *The Rite of Confirmation*, Introduction ¶5; see also Canon 893 §2. The Introduction goes on to say that the option of choosing a special sponsor for confirmation is not excluded. Even the parents themselves may present their children for confirmation – depending on what the local Ordinary determines.

14 *The Catechism*, ¶1309.

15 Some ideas of community work include

- helping at home without being asked to do so – things like setting the table, clearing away, helping to prepare meals, cleaning the house or taking the dog for a walk
- visiting the sick or elderly, helping housebound people with shopping or other errands
- offering time and help to a local Good Neighbour Scheme
- reading at Mass or serving as a Eucharistic Minister
- volunteering to join in the music at Mass by playing a musical instrument or by singing
- joining local justice and peace groups or groups working for ecology or third world needs.

The candidates must be suitably disposed and instructed

Canon law tells us that the candidates must be properly disposed and suitably instructed to celebrate the sacrament.[16]

What does this mean? Let's look at three ways the candidates will show they are ready:

- The candidates should be willing to celebrate the sacrament.
  This will include a desire on the part of the candidate to participate fully in the programme of preparation and to celebrate the sacrament with a reverence and appreciation appropriate to his/her age.
- The candidate should be aware of belonging to the Catholic community through baptism. Jesus invites us into intimacy with himself and he invites us to follow him. If the candidate sees that call as relevant and meaningful in their life by acting with compassion, justice and mercy, it shows their readiness.
- The candidate should be regularly attending Mass on Sundays with a level of understanding of the Mass commensurate with his/her ability.

The requirement that the candidate be suitably instructed reflects the concern which led to the institution of the catechumenate in the early Church and, indeed, to its restoration in our own time for the initiation of adults into the faith and life of the Church.

The Catechism tells us that candidates should celebrate the sacrament of reconciliation by way of their preparation.[17] Many of these young people will not be celebrating the sacrament of reconciliation regularly; doing so in preparation for the confirmation may give them a positive experience they will look back on – and one that will encourage them to realise how relevant this sacrament is in their lives.

Catechesis for confirmation should take place in the parish

We are told that, as with baptism, catechesis for confirmation should take place within the parish community – since it is the faith community into whose life of prayer and worship the candidates will be more fully initiated.[18]

Our programme suggests two liturgical rites which take place during Sunday Masses when the community comes together to pray and to worship. Confirmation is an important event in the life of the parish community and the parish needs to be aware of and be involved in their preparation. The celebrations also offer an important opportunity for the young people to feel a part of the community, celebrating and praying with the community they are to be more fully initiated into.

There must be 'content' in the catechesis

We define 'content' as something contained in (such as the table of contents).
It might also be defined it as something expressed through a medium such as music, literature or art.

So, where do we find 'content' in catechesis? Well, the General Directory for Catechesis tells us that the kind of growth in Christian life we have been talking about is achieved in the following ways

16 *Code of Canon Law*, Collins Liturgical Publications, London, 1983, Canon 889 §2.

17 *The Catechism*, ¶1310.

18 *The Rite of Confirmation*, ¶11.

- in Scripture
- through witness (or apostolic work)
- in our Creed (our profession of faith)
- through our lived moral values
- and in our liturgies and in our prayer[19]

In fact, the Catechism of the Catholic Church is structured around these same fundamental dimensions (or pillars) of the Christian life:

- the profession of faith
- the celebration of the liturgy and the sacraments
- morality of the Gospel and
- prayer[20]

I believe that, in catechesis, Jesus is the content – and we come to know Jesus through the mediums of *scripture*, through *witness*, through our *lived moral values* and *in our liturgies* and *in our prayer*. This programme is based on those mediums.

The programme

The programme begins with a session called 'Our search for God and God's search for us.'[21] Our search for God has been expressed from the beginning of time, but Christianity has its starting point in the Incarnation of the Word. Here, it is not simply a case of our seeking God, but of God who seeks us so much that he comes in person to speak to us and to tell us what he is like. To help us to understand, we hear two scripture stories Jesus told. He taught us what God is like by telling stories which have a clear and vivid point. The meaning is not explained but is left for us to work out for ourselves. Like the story of the walk to Emmaus, he always lets us decide for ourselves.

Every session should begin and end with a prayer. Every session has a theme and scripture and every session invites a response – or sends us out with a message for our lives. I suggest you follow this format:

- *Begin with a prayer.* You may use the one on the following pages, you may prepare a prayer that suits the session or you may prefer to pray spontaneously.
- *Introduce the theme for the session.* Tell the young people what the theme or the aim of the session is.
- *Life's experience.* Ask the young people to talk in two's or three's about some aspect in their own life's experience relating to the theme of the session. I've included a story at the beginning of each session to help them think of something. Better still, use my story to get an idea of a story of your own and tell your story to get them started.

19 *General Directory of Catechesis*, Congregation for the Clergy, Catholic Truth Society, London, 1997, ¶¶94-95 and 117-119. See also the Rite of Christian Initiation of Adults, ¶¶75.1-75.4.

20 *The Catechism* as quoted in ¶122 of the General Directory of Catechesis.

21 See also ¶26 of the *Catechism*.

- *Listen to God's Word.* Proclaim the Scripture. Read it with understanding and read it well. Then, one of the catechists should briefly 'break this open', i.e., explain it to the group in a way they can relate to. Or, tell them about a Tradition of the Church and explain that.
  To help to make it their own,

- *Break into groups* of no more than six people (including a catechist) and reflect. You may want to talk – answering the questions offered in the session; or

- *You may prefer to have an activity* to help people get the message.

- *Draw out the message.* You may do this in your small group discussion or you may try to get feedback. The 'message' has, hopefully, come from the young people. It is important to let them tell you what it is.

- *Finish the session with a prayer* – or a reflection – which pulls together what the session has aimed to do.

Each of these steps is important in your session – although you can change the order around. You can listen to the Scripture (or Tradition) first and then ask people to reflect on their life's experience. Some people try to incorporate a link with life experience into the discussion. I find that asking people to talk in two's or three's at the beginning of the session is a way of breaking the ice and making people feel more comfortable – and, having done that, they are more inclined to share in the group discussions later.

Mark the importance of noting what the theme or the aim of the session is. Educators tell us that this helps all the participants focus on what they are trying to accomplish in the session. Notice how I suggest you do this in five places:

- at the beginning of the session when you introduce the theme,
- when you read the Word (or tell them about the Tradition), and then,
- when you break open the Word (or Tradition),
- when you draw out the message from the young people,
- and, again, when you conclude the session.

Mark, too, the importance of keeping the session flowing. The prayer and the introduction of the theme take only a few minutes. Sharing life experience, again, takes only a few minutes – depending on how the conversations are going. The reading of Scripture and the input should take 5-7 minutes. Keep the input brief. Prepare it well and present it in such a way that it makes people think about what God is saying to them – in such a way that it stimulates discussion within the small groups or helps to make the activity make sense. There is enough material in the sessions for a new or inexperienced (or even a busy) catechist to follow; and it will work well. However, the more you make the material your own, the more you an draw on your own experience, the better it will work.

This book is divided into sections:

- first, this introduction section
- the enquiry sessions
- two celebration Masses
- the catechetical sessions
- the final (prayerful) preparation sessions and
- a post-confirmation session

There are also ideas for a day of recollection and for a service of reconciliation and, in the appendix, there are liturgy sheets for the celebrations (which may be photocopied for use by the group using this programme.)

This introduction

This introduction aims to help the catechist understand the programme. It has a proven track record and it works. I urge you to follow the programme structure. More experienced catechists will adapt the material – using the notes for the catechists to help them to see one way of getting the theme across – and deciding whether they want to use different scripture readings and prayers which are more appropriate to their own group.

Some groups follow the lectionary and use the Sunday readings for their sessions. Once you have agreed the schedule for your programme, check the readings of the day for each of the sessions. You may be surprised to see how the readings fit into the programme. Do not be afraid to switch the order of the sessions around (particularly during the catechetical period) if you see that the readings are appropriate to the themes of the sessions. If you can adapt the session to incorporate the readings of the day, it will help the candidates to see how God speaks to us in Scripture today in our lives. Remember what I have said: the more you make the material your own, the better you will be able to facilitate the session for the young people. The more you enter into the experience yourself, the more you will be challenged and the more you will grow in your own faith.

The enquiry period

This is a time of enquiry, not of commitment. It is, perhaps, the most difficult one to handle. It is a time when the young people can observe and question the meaning in their lives. They bring their own stories and their own questions about their stories. They may ask if Jesus and the Church say anything to these questions.

The Mass of Enrolment

The enquiry period leads to the Mass of Enrolment – when the young people say, 'yes, I am willing to be enrolled in the programme to be prepared for the sacrament of confirmation' – and they now become candidates. Their parents and the parish community are asked if they are willing to support and guide the young people by their prayers and example.

The catechetical period

This is the central period of the programme. It is a time when they learn more about Christ – discovering what difference it makes in the decisions they make in their lives if they are to be his followers. They should turn more readily to God in prayer, to bear witness to the faith, to keep their hopes set on Christ, follow the inspiration of the Holy Spirit and practice love of neighbour.[22] This is the time when they reflect on what it means to be a Catholic Christian, a time when they should be involved in their community projects.[23] By the time they finish this period and they are ready for the Mass of Commitment, they should have sponsors to accompany them on their journey.[24]

The Mass of Commitment

The catechetical period leads to the Mass of Commitment – when the candidates say they understand the importance of what they are doing and say, 'yes, I am willing to continue to take part conscientiously in the remainder of the programme.' They pray for a deeper growth in faith and hope and love and their parents and the parish community are asked if they are willing to continue to support the candidates.

The final (prayerful) preparation period

This period is quite different from the preceding periods. If confirmations take place during the Easter season, this period often coincides with Lent. It is intended to be a time of retreat – with the emphasis on prayer and spiritual preparation for the sacrament of confirmation rather than on study and learning. This period is not one of learning about Christ so much as reflecting on these personal encounters with him.

It is during this period that the candidates prepare to renew their baptismal promises – reflecting on what they believe in. It is now, perhaps, that they experience the Mass in a new way; and it is now that they may go away for a weekend retreat or have a day of recollection.

Post-Confirmation

The post-confirmation period begins immediately after the young people have celebrated the sacrament of confirmation. They face the prospect of living out the Christian life day by day. About a month after the confirmation, meet with the young people offering them the chance to reflect on what they have learned during the programme of preparation and what they have experienced in the celebration of the sacrament.

The newly confirmed young people should be helped to grow into the local community; they should be reminded how important they are to the community. This is, of course, a two-way thing; but the community should give them thoughtful and friendly help and should make it clear that they are welcome.

22 *RCIA*, ¶75.2.

23 *The Rite of Confirmation*, Introduction ¶3 tells us that catechesis for confirmation should strive to awaken a sense of belonging to the Church of Jesus Christ, the universal Church as well as the parish community.

24 Canon 892 says that the sponsor or godparent should know the candidate well enough to testify that they behave as true witnesses of Christ.

Some suggestions about setting up the programme:

Long-term preparation (up to a year in advance):

- Set the date for the Confirmation with the Bishop and with the church. (In Westminster Diocese, Confirmations take place between Easter and Pentecost.)
- Book the date for the residential retreat or day(s) of recollection.
- Plan the schedule of the programme with the catechists (preparation sessions, candidates sessions, parents' sessions and liturgies) around the date of the Confirmation and the retreat.
- Recruit and commence training of catechists if necessary.

Medium-plan preparation (just before and during the programme):

- Introduction for candidates, parents and, if possible, sponsors between two weeks and a month before programme begins.
- Candidates' sessions 1-3 (period of enquiry) and, perhaps, a day of recollection
- Mass of Enrolment
- Candidates' sessions 4-8 (period of catechesis)
- Mass of Commitment
- Candidates' sessions 9-10 (period of prayerful preparation) and a day of recollection or a retreat
- Practice for Confirmation
- Celebration of the Sacrament of Confirmation

Afterwards (within a month of the Confirmation):

- Conclude the programme; ask for comments and offer the newly confirmed young people an opportunity to reflect on what they have learned and what they have experienced in the celebration of the sacrament. You can combine this with a party!
- Catechists' evaluation and celebration.

Some suggestions about running the programme:

Preparation is important

- A one-hour session often takes up to two hours of preparation – so factor this time into your schedule. It is said that how well your session goes and how well you hold the attention of the candidates is directly related to how well you have planned the session.

- It is good to share your preparation time with the other catechists involved if at all possible; working together is fun, it is challenging and it is a wonderful opportunity to grow in your own faith. Remember, the more you have entered into the theme of the session and the more you have practised verbalising it, the easier it will be to present it to the candidates and to talk to the candidates in the small groups.

- Whoever is going to give the input, to break open the Word, must be well-prepared. All the catechists can help 'brainstorm' at the preparation session.

This will help the one who is giving the input and it will help the other team members lead their small groups in discussion. The notes in each session will give you some ideas to get you started. There is plenty of material available to help you; look at other confirmation programmes, read books and copy good ideas you notice in other catechists.

Evaluation is also important

- At the end of every session, take some time (10-15 minutes) to talk with the other catechists, asking what went well and what did not go well. What do we definitely want to do again and what did we learn from what went wrong? Try to be as honest as you can with one another. If someone was not speaking clearly, say so. They will not improve if they don't know that people could not understand what they were saying. If someone took too long to get the point across, say so. We cannot afford to lose the candidates' attention (and it will throw out the time plan for the session). And if someone did really well – their input was inspiring or they dealt with a tricky situation well – say that too! It is important to make the criticisms constructive and to accept both the criticisms and the compliments gracefully.

Share the work!

- The catechists should share the responsibilities – so, for example
- one person may be responsible for collecting baptism certificates (and any money you may ask for towards the books, retreat or day(s) of recollection, etc.) This may be the same person who takes note of the attendance.
- one or two people may be responsible to arrange the chairs where you meet before the candidates arrive.
- one person may be responsible for providing a centrepiece or a focal point – perhaps a low small table with a white cloth, a candle, a crucifix and an open Bible on it.
- If you offer drinks and snacks, one person may take responsibility for that.
- You might ask parishioners to pray for the candidates, to sponsor bibles (if you give them to the candidates), etc.

Communicate!

- If your parish priest is not on the team, keep him informed of how things are going.
- Always prepare liturgies far enough in advance so that you can
  - show them to the priest who will be presiding at the liturgy,
  - make sure those who are involved in the music ministry know what is happening, have a chance to practice, etc. and
  - organise readers, eucharistic ministers, collectors and someone to bring the offertory gifts forward. (Always make sure you tell those who are normally the readers, eucharistic ministers, etc. at this Sunday Mass that something different is happening.)

- Keep the parents informed of what is happening, give them a copy of the schedule and, if you take the candidates away for a retreat or day(s) of recollection, make sure you get their written permission.

This programme is not a crash course in Catholicism

There is a tendency at times to think that the confirmation candidates must know everything that the Catholic Church teaches. This is unrealistic! We need to nurture the recognition that being a Christian requires lifelong learning – and different kinds of learning at different times in our lives.

Baptism, confirmation and the eucharist are considered to be the sacraments of initiation – so called because it is through them that we become Christians. The catechesis offered in this programme should be complete enough for an intelligent and well-prepared sacrament of initiation; but it should be recognised as one stage in an on-going catechesis.

Remember, too, that the parents are the principal educators of their children in the ways of faith. While it is important that the developing independence of the young people is respected, it should not be forgotten that the home is still the most significant *school of faith*. Sacramental preparation is complementary to what happens in our families; it is also complementary to the religious education offered in our Catholic schools and the religious education programmes offered in parishes for those who do not attend Catholic schools.

Parents' sessions

Every effort should be made to affirm the parents for all the good work they have done. Parents often appreciate the opportunity of hearing what is happening in their children's preparation for confirmation. Many parents have not had much of an opportunity to be catechised (other than coming to Mass). Some parents will not be attending Mass regularly; some will feel excluded because they are single, separated or divorced and some may be in irregular marital situations. Some parents may not be Catholic and some may have special needs.

Parents' sessions offer an opportunity of meeting the parents where they are, making them feel welcome and supporting them in their role as their children's teachers of faith.

Be aware of the law

It is important that catechists are aware of the laws relating to working with young people. Find out what the Child Protection Policy is in your diocese and comply with it.

Equally, find out what health and safety regulations apply to the place where you meet; know where the fire exits are, know where the first aid kit is and where the accident book is.

Pray

Above all pray! Pray for the candidates and pray that the Holy Spirit will speak through you. Enjoy the programme!

Diana Klein

Prayer

We begin each session with a prayer

We begin each session by remembering that we are in God's presence.
You might use this prayer at the beginning of each session
– adopting it as your programme prayer,
or you might find another prayer you think appropriate to your session.
Even better, you might make up a prayer yourself.

We light a candle to remind us
that throughout the Old Testament
God promised us a light in our darkness.
We believe that Jesus is that light
and the candle helps us to remember
Jesus is present with us.

Jesus, you promised that
where two or three come together in your name,
you would be there with them.[25]
We are here in your name;
help us to notice you in our midst.
We turn to you and ask for the gift of your Spirit.
Lead us and guide us as we prepare to be confirmed. Amen

25 Matthew 18:20.

Enquiry Sessions

SESSION 1

Introduction to the programme

We begin the session with a prayer

The aims of this session are:

- to feel welcome and at home
- introduce the catechists and the candidates to one another
- to find out about the programme

Getting to know one another

HERE are a couple of ice breakers – fun ways of helping the catechists and the candidates to introduce themselves and to begin to know each other's names:

- Take away one chair from the circle; the person without a chair stands in the middle of the circle and says, "My name is "X" and I like people with, for example, black shoes." Everyone with black shoes must move to another chair; this cannot be the chair they were sitting next to or the chair they were sitting in. It becomes riotous when the person in the middle says they like people with ears or hair and everyone has to move! After ten minutes, you will know the names of some of the group and people will be sitting next to new people.
- Make up a questionnaire – perhaps ten questions, questions like:
  - What is your favourite activity?
  - Who is your favourite actor or actress? your favourite singer?
  - What is your favourite book? or film? or subject at school?
  - What was your favourite holiday?
  - What is your favourite food? or your least favourite food?
  - What is the most outrageous thing you've ever done?
  - What is the most fun, the riskiest, the silliest, the cleverest thing you've ever done?

  You might make up a form leaving space for the answers. Each question must be asked of a different person – and, depending on the size of the group and how well they know each other, you might say they have to ask people they don't know. They must ask the person's name and write down the answer. Again, it is a good way to get to know the names of some of the group.

A note for the candidates about the programme[26]

The time of preparation for the sacrament of confirmation is a special time, a time of friendship, a time of discoveries – about our faith in God, about ourselves, and about our community. Most young people are confirmed as teenagers; and most of you were baptised as infants. It was your parents and godparents who spoke on your behalf at that time. Now it is time for you to speak for yourself – to declare what you believe. It is about your choice to be followers of Christ.

In all cultures, there are formal and informal rituals to initiate new members, to express who belongs. Christians have the sacraments of initiation to signify and celebrate those who have heard the gospel message and have become disciples – sharing in the mission of the Church, with both the privileges and the responsibilities that come from belonging.

...it is time for you to speak for yourself... to declare what you believe

Like baptism and the eucharist, confirmation is a sacrament of initiation. We believe that each of the rites of initiation is an expression of commitment to the process of becoming adult Christians – or Christian adults. I pray that during this programme, you will be open to the Holy Spirit, that you will decide to be initiated as a full member of the Church. I also pray that this time of preparation will help you to deepen your relationship with Jesus and your understanding of the call to be his followers – seeing that this call is relevant, meaningful and fulfilling in your lives.

This call for commitment is not something that just happens on the day you are confirmed; it is something that continues. We do not only say, 'yes, I want to be committed' the day we are confirmed; we say, 'yes, I am willing to be committed; I am willing to be more and more like you, Jesus' every time we celebrate His greatest gift to us, the Eucharist.

confirmation is a sacrament of initiation

During this time of preparation, we look at our own life experiences; we listen to God – either in Scripture or the Tradition of the Church or in Church teaching; and then we get a message for our own lives. We reflect on the meaning of life and we look at our response to the values we discover. One of the ways we respond is by using the gifts we have and getting involved in some aspect of community work. Here are some ideas how you might get involved:

...deepen your relationship with Jesus and your understanding of the call to be his followers...

- You can help at home without being asked to do so – things like setting the table, clearing away, helping to prepare meals, cleaning the house or taking the dog for a walk.
- You might visit the sick or elderly.
- You might help housebound people with shopping or other errands.
- If you are handy, you might volunteer to make minor repairs or garden for people who cannot do these things themselves.
- You might offer time and help to a local Good Neighbour Scheme.
- If you are good at football, you might volunteer to coach primary school children.

26 © Diana Klein 2002. Multiple copies of this note (pages 18-19) may be made by the purchasing church group for the candidates using this programme.

- If you are thinking about being a teacher, you might consider helping with the First Communion preparation in the parish.
- If you are concerned about the homeless, you might consider helping at a shelter or with a soup run.
- If you are a good reader, you might like to read at Mass; or, you might offer to be a Eucharistic Minister.
- If you are musical, you might volunteer to join in the music at Mass – by playing a musical instrument or by singing.
- If you are interested in issues of peace and justice, or in ecology or in third world needs, you might like to raise funds and donate them to a charity of your choice.

you will need a sponsor

As you prepare to be confirmed, you will be invited to different ways of praying. You might find some of the ways of praying new to you – new ways to respond to God – in conversation, in reflection, in meditations.

involve your sponsor in this time of preparation

At your confirmation, you will need a sponsor. This might be one of your godparents; it should be the kind of person you can go to when you want to discuss spiritual and moral issues in your lives. You should choose your sponsor carefully and involve your sponsor in this time of preparation for the sacrament. They are asked to stand as witnesses to your moral character, faith and intention to make a Christian commitment. Therefore, they should be people who know you and who can help you grow in your attitude to become a mature, responsible, committed (that is confirmed) member of the Church, a follower of Jesus. Your sponsor must be a baptised and confirmed Catholic, who is regularly receiving the Eucharist (and must be over the age of 16).

choose a name which will mean something to you

You may chose a confirmation name if you wish in addition to your baptismal name. It is important to choose a name which will mean something to you. Your confirmation name must be the name of a saint. You should be inspired by the example of the saint whose name you choose; and, during the course, you might pray to this saint for guidance and help.

Diana Klein

Enquiry Sessions

SESSION 2

Our search for God and God's search for us

We begin the session with a prayer

The aims of this session are:

- to think about how we search for God in our lives.
- to realise that God searches for us too. He searches so much for us that he came in person to tell us what he is like. That person, Jesus, described himself as the way, the truth and the life.[27] We have at the heart of our faith a person. This makes Christianity different from other religions.

Looking at our life experience

What is the truth?

WHAT is the truth? Why is it important? What is reality? We all have these questions – in all cultures, at all ages.

Is the truth important to you?

I remember reading the same story reported in three different newspapers. I was shocked to see how differently it was reported in each of them. How on earth can you tell which is true? Each of the journalists had looked at the story from their own point of view and the way they told the story coloured my impression of what had really happened. I had always thought that newspapers had to tell the truth! Which was true, I wondered?

Do you think newspapers tell the truth? Is the truth important to you? Why not take a look at some newspapers for yourself and compare how the same story is reported in three different newspapers?

27 John 14:6.

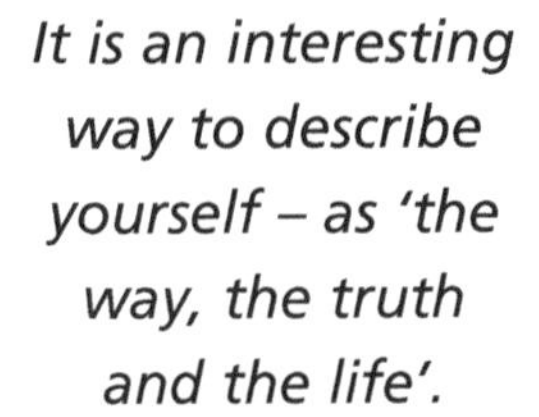

You might think about what truth is most important to you.

- the truth you tell your parents? or the truth they tell you?
- the truth you tell your friends?
- the truth they tell you? or the truth you tell yourself?

We listen to Scripture

Jesus described himself as 'the way, the truth and the life'.[28] We have at the heart of our faith a person. This makes Christianity different from other religions. Our search for God has been expressed from the beginning of time; but Christianity has its starting-point in the Incarnation of the Word. Here, it is not simply a case of our seeking God, but of God who seeks us so much that he comes in person to speak to us and to tell us what he is like.

We have at the heart of our faith a person

It is an interesting way to describe yourself – as 'the way, *the truth* and the life'. What was Jesus telling us about his identity? I think this was one of the ways that he told us that he had come to tell us about God; and he did it by telling stories which have a point. However, he never explains the meaning; to some extent, he leaves us to work it out for ourselves. For example, he told a couple of stories about people searching:

It is an interesting way to describe yourself – as 'the way, the truth and the life'.

The first one is about a shepherd with a hundred sheep who loses one:

"Which one of you, having a hundred sheep and losing one of them, does not leave the ninety-nine in the wilderness and go after the one that is lost until he finds it? When he has found it, he lays it on his shoulders and rejoices. And when he comes home, he calls together his friends and neighbours, saying to them, 'Rejoice with me, for I have found my sheep that was lost.' "[29]

Why was Jesus telling this story? Was it to say how good the shepherd was to go and find the lost sheep? It seems a bit strange (even irresponsible) that the shepherd leaves the other ninety-nine sheep in the wilderness to go and find one lost sheep. Despite the fact that the sheep is stupid and gets lost, the shepherd cares about it; he picks it up – smelly and probably very muddy as it was – and lays it on his shoulders. And, Jesus tells us that when the shepherd found the lost sheep, he celebrates with all his friends and neighbours.

The second story is about a woman who loses a coin:

"Or what woman having ten silver coins, if she loses one of them, does not light a lamp, sweep the house, and search carefully until she finds it? When she has found it, she calls together her friends and neighbours, saying, 'Rejoice with me, for I have found the coin that I had lost.' "[30]

28 John 14:6.
29 Luke 15:4-6.
30 Luke 15:8-9.

Here is a woman who spends so much energy finding her lost coin. This story makes almost the same point as the first one. However, instead of a moderately rich shepherd – which we assume he is since he has a hundred sheep – we have a poor woman who has lost a large amount of her money. In this case, the coin is passive – it's just a coin; but the woman is so eager to find it and how joyful she is when she does.

Questions for group discussion

- Have you ever lost something important to you and searched for it as caringly as this shepherd or as eagerly as this woman?
- When you found it, how did you feel? Did you celebrate?
- Can you see what message Jesus is trying to tell us?
- Do you think Jesus might be saying that this man and this woman – in the way they searched for the sheep and the coin – were in some way like God in the way he searches for us?

What message do we get?

God wants us all in his kingdom

Perhaps Jesus is telling us in these stories that God wants us all in his kingdom – no matter who we are. We might be like the lost sheep – smelly, dirty and a bit dumb. We might be like the lost coin – something that doesn't appear to be worth a lot to others, but worth a great deal to the woman. Maybe he is telling us that God searches for us whatever we are like and he delights in finding us.

Jesus gives his followers a mission of love that goes beyond any other love.

On the other hand, maybe Jesus is telling us that God is like the man in the first story and like the woman in the second story – and Jesus is inviting us to be like God and to be like this man and this woman. He gives his followers a mission of love that goes beyond any other love[31] – a mission to go out and search for those who are lost, those who need help, those who need to be found. Perhaps these stories tell us about the kind of compassionate love Jesus wants his followers to have for others.

We pray

Gracious and loving God,
we thank you for bringing us together
as we search for you in our lives.
Each of us belongs to a family;
each of us also belongs to wider communities –
at school, in our parishes and where we live.
We journey together searching for meaning,
inspired by one another and by our stories.
Christians belong to the community which is the Church.
As we journey together reflecting on what it is to be a follower of Christ,
help us and inspire us to commit ourselves
to the mission of love that goes beyond other love.
We ask this through Christ, our Lord. Amen.

---

31 See Luke 14:25-35 where Jesus talks about the total commitment which is at the heart of one's life that makes true followers of Jesus.

Enquiry Sessions

Prayer

SESSION 3

We begin the session with a prayer

The aims of this session are:

- to recognise our need to pray and to look at some different kinds of prayer.
- to realise that we are invited to pray with others – and, sometimes, to share with others what happens in our prayer.

Looking at our life experience

WHEN I was a child, I dreamt about having a horse. I was living in New York City, though, and there wasn't much chance of having a horse there! I spent my time reading books about horses and imagining what it would be like to own a horse. When I came to London as a young adult, one of the first things I did was to learn how to ride; and, eventually, I bought a horse. I can vividly remember what it was like.

I loved this horse so much – all I wanted to do was to spend time with her, riding her and grooming her. I learned how to take care of her needs and didn't mind all the hard work that goes with taking care of a horse.

I couldn't believe I was so lucky to own a horse. My horse knew me and knew just what I needed from her. We were able to communicate in a way beyond what language allows. With me, she was gentle; she was kind to me and I felt safe with her. With others, however, she would sometimes be quite wild. She didn't like slightly built men – and was known to dump them in a puddle if they tried to ride her!

Think about what it is like when you love someone, how you communicate it.

- You say you love them or communicate in some way.
- You want to be with them, to spend time with them.
- You are happy, thankful they are there.
- You can tell them what your needs, your desires are.
- You respond to them when they ask you to do something, when they tell you their needs.

Prayer is communication with God in the same way

Some days you feel you have to pray.

Some days you feel you have to pray. Something deep inside you seems to direct you to pray. Maybe something wonderful has happened and you are incredibly grateful; you might even say, 'Thank God!' Other times, you feel particularly helpless or inadequate and this makes you feel you should turn to God to ask for help or just to say, 'Help!' And, sometimes, someone you love is suffering or something awful has happened and you ask God, 'Why? How could you let this happen?' Prayer comes spontaneously; it seems the only thing to do.

Prayer may be difficult if you haven't really learned to pray or if you have abandoned prayer, and you may feel strange – embarrassed almost – to pray. Sometimes people continue to pray as they did when they learned as a small child. Their prayer hasn't changed as they have grown older; it doesn't fit with their current experience of life. For others, prayer is just a kind of routine, something they 'do' every so often. It consists of a series of requests or memorised prayers that they don't think about very much, or, perhaps, don't understand or expect much from – certainly not much like a conversation with a friend.

You need to pray in the way that you can.

On the other hand, people sometimes experience difficulty with prayer because they expect too much. They expect, for example, to feel good every time they pray; or they may expect something magical to happen – and it doesn't. Prayer, for them, is asking a favour of God (for something they can't do themselves) and expecting immediate results, like saying a frantic prayer during a test and expecting God to give them the answer for something they didn't study for! For them, prayer is going to God in desperation. It is what I call the God of the bubble gum machine; you put the coin in and get the bubble gum out. These people expect to put the prayer in and get the result out!

You need to pray in the way that you can. There are a lot of different styles, starting points. You could try silence, you could try to find time and space to be alone, you might repeat a mantra over and over again. You might try to use your imagination – and imagine yourself being in the gospel stories. Be willing and God will lead you on.

Take the time to look back on what is happening in your life.

Take the time to look back on what is happening in your life. Look back over what is happening in your life and see where God has been. You might find it helpful to do this each day – perhaps before you go to sleep. Think about all the good things you have seen, done, felt. Think about all the good things that have happened to you. Think about the times when you have appreciated what someone has done for you. Think about the love you felt for others and the love you felt from others. How grateful are you to God for all that you are and all that you have? Think, too, about where things have gone wrong; where you have not done something good that you could have done during the day. Think about what you learned from your mistakes and know that God loves you.

We will specially use two kinds of prayer during this course

Prayer of contemplation – when we enter into a life event or story passage of Scripture as if we were there. We enter by way of imagination, making use of all our senses. The Spirit of God leads us. In contemplation,

- we watch what happens in the Scripture story and we listen to what is being said.
- we might assume the role of one of the persons in the story.
- we look at each of the people involved and wonder what they are experiencing. Who are they speaking to? How are they feeling? and
- we ask what God is saying to us.

Centering prayer – In centering prayer, we go beyond thought and image, beyond the senses and the rational mind to that centre of our being where God is working. It is a very simple, pure form of prayer – frequently without words – it is an opening of our hearts to the Spirit dwelling within us. We find a place of stillness within us.

Scripture tells us

St. Paul said, "The Spirit comes to help us in our weakness... the Spirit... expresses our pleas in a way that could never be put into words..."[32] He talked about how the Spirit of Jesus within us cries out "Abba, Father!"[33]

In this session, we will try a centering prayer. Take a comfortable posture. Close your eyes. I invite you to keep silent for a few minutes. First, you will try to attain silence, a silence as total as you can – in your heart and your mind. Be aware of the noises around you and let them be. Just be still. We read in the psalms: "Be still and know that I am God..."[34]

Be aware of how you are feeling – of all the sensations in your body, which you are not explicitly aware of. Be aware of your clothing touching your body. Be aware of how your head is feeling resting on your shoulders. Be aware of your back resting on the chair, and your arms, and your hands resting on your lap. Now, be aware of your legs as they rest on the chair, of your feet in your shoes. Take a breath in and hold it for a moment or two. Now let it go and, with it, let go of any anxiety or tension you have. Then, breathe in all the goodness and love of God. Repeat this a few times. Pause for a moment and realise that you are dependent on God for your every breath.

We are going to take a walk in a nearby park. It is a beautiful afternoon and you are on your own. Walk down the path, noticing the time of the year and how warm or how cold it is. As you enter the park, choose a path you would like to follow. Notice how the park smells today, how the sun is shining on the

32 Romans 8:26.
33 Romans 8:15.
34 Psalm 46:10.

grass. Walk through the park and listen to the birds singing; hear the gentle wind blowing in the trees. As you are walking along, you can hear in the near distance some running water – perhaps a stream – and you go to find it. What is it like? Is it wide or narrow, deep or shallow; is the water running quickly over heavy stones? There is a tree stump just beside the stream and you decide to sit down for a while – just taking in the beauty, the sun glistening on the stream.

A few minutes later, you notice someone walking towards you. You don't know how, but you know that this is Jesus. What does he look like? What is he wearing? Is he wearing a long white robe and sandals – or is he wearing jeans and a sweatshirt? Does he have long hair and a beard – or short hair? What colour is his hair? What colour is his skin?

Jesus comes and greets you. What does he say? You begin a conversation with him. Remain with it for a few minutes. Tell him about yourself and ask him about himself. Tell him what is important to you; ask him what he cares most about. After a few minutes, Jesus says goodbye to you and leaves. You rest for a few minutes reflecting on what has just happened. Then you hear someone else calling you. You meet them and leave the park.

Some questions for group discussion

- Have you ever prayed like this? Did you like it?
- Could you see what Jesus was wearing? What was it?
- What did Jesus say to you? and what did you say to him?
- Is it important to share what happened in our prayer?

What message do we get?

There is something in us that draws us into prayer – and we need different kinds of prayer at different times. We need to pray on our own and sometimes we need to share with others what has happened in our prayer. Telling one another what happens often brings our prayer alive.

We also need to pray in our parish community and with our families. We need to pray with the young and the old, with the weak and the strong in our parishes – the community we are being initiated into. We also need to observe others praying. Many people say that they learned how to pray by watching their parents pray. This, they say, is how they were drawn into prayer – aware somehow that their parent was engaged in something special, something sacred, something they, too, wanted to experience.

We pray

May the God of our Lord Jesus Christ,
the Father of glory,
give us a spirit of wisdom and perception of what is revealed,
to bring us to full knowledge of him.
May he enlighten the eyes of our minds
so that we can see what hope his call holds for us,
what rich glories he has promised we will inherit
and how infinitely great is the power
that he has exercised for us believers.[35]

35 Adaptation of Ephesians 1:17-19 to make a prayer.

Celebration 1

CELEBRATION 1

Mass of Enrolment

The enquiry period has now come to an end. It has been a time of enquiry for you, not of commitment. If you express a desire to continue to be prepared to be confirmed, you are ready for the Mass of Enrolment.

This celebration is important for you. So that it is clear that this decision to continue is made freely by you, you will be asked in the presence of the parish community if you want to be enrolled – as candidates – in the programme to be prepared for the sacrament of confirmation.

Your parents and the parish community will be asked if they are willing to support and guide you by their prayers and example. By doing this, the parents and the parish community realise the responsibilities they have towards you as you prepare to be confirmed.

At the beginning of the Mass, the priest will probably want to welcome you, your catechists, parents (and sponsors, if they can come) in a special way – explaining what this Mass of Enrolment is about.

After the Gospel, you will be presented to the parish community by a catechist. In some parishes, the questions are included in a Mass booklet which includes the readings of the day and hymns which will be sung at that Mass.[36]

Catechist 'Father, I am here to present to the parish community the young people of our parish who have asked to join our programme to be prepared for the sacrament of confirmation.

The priest addresses the young people, saying 'My young friends, do you want to be enrolled in the programme to be prepared for the sacrament of confirmation?' They reply 'We do.'

He asks their parents: 'Are you willing to support these young people as they prepare for the sacrament of confirmation?'
They reply, 'We do.'

36 You will find a simple booklet in the appendix which you can use although you might want to do a more personalised booklet which includes the hymns and references to the readings of the Sunday.

He then asks the parish community: 'Are you willing to support and pray for these candidates by your prayers and example?'
They reply, 'We are.'

He concludes by addressing the young people: 'The parish community welcomes you with great joy. You are now enrolled as candidates. May God bless you as you begin your preparations for the sacrament of confirmation.'

Catechetical Sessions

SESSION 4

The Gifts of the Spirit

We begin the session with a prayer.

The aims of this session are:

- to become more aware of the gifts of the Holy Spirit in us – and
- to see how we can use these gifts for the service of one another.

Looking at our life experience

Let's think about the kind of gifts we receive. Broadly speaking, there are two kinds of gifts we receive:

- those we want and use, those that mean something special to us and
- those we put aside until a time when we can get rid of them

nothing is impossible

WHEN I was about 10 or 11 years old, I asked for ice skates as a Christmas gift. My mother was not happy! She was convinced that ice skating was dangerous and she was afraid I would break a leg or my neck or something. Furthermore, we didn't know anyone who could teach me how to skate and I certainly could not skate if I hadn't been taught to. On the other hand, I was equally convinced. I was certain I could ice skate; I thought that if I could roller skate, I should be able to ice skate and I was right. When my godmother gave me the ice skates I so wanted,
I put them on and I skated! It was not a problem! Shortly afterwards, my mother bought me a little gift – a very small gold case with a plastic dome with a mustard seed inside. On the back, in tiny letters, I found the story Jesus told of the mustard seed – the one where he says that you need faith only the size of a mustard seed and nothing is impossible.[37]
How appropriate! Now, this little gift has become one of my most precious possessions – not just because it happened to be appropriate on that occasion, but because it says something important about me.

Think about a gift you have received which says something about you.

37 Matthew 17:20.

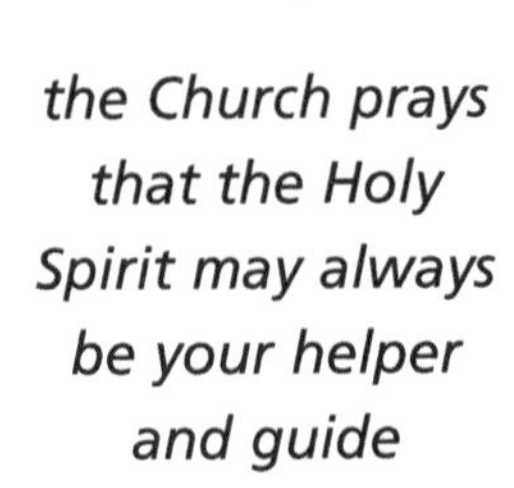

At your Confirmation,

the Church prays that the Holy Spirit may always be your helper and guide. We pray that you may receive all the gifts of the Holy Spirit to help you live as a Christian and to help to build God's kingdom. This is the prayer the bishop or priest says as he holds his hands over you in blessing:

> All powerful God, Father of our Lord Jesus Christ,
> By water and the Holy Spirit
> you freed your sons and daughters from sin and gave them new life.
> Send your Holy Spirit upon them to be their helper and guide.
> Give them the spirit of wisdom and understanding,
> the gift of right judgement and courage,
> the spirit of knowledge and reverence.
> Fill them with the spirit of wonder and awe in your presence.
> We ask this through Christ our Lord.

the Church prays that the Holy Spirit may always be your helper and guide

This prayer is based on a Scripture reading from Isaiah.[38]

> There shall come forth a shoot from the stump of Jesse
> And a blossom shall spring from his roots.
> And, the spirit of the LORD shall rest on him,
> the spirit of wisdom and understanding,
> the spirit of counsel and might,
> the spirit of knowledge and the fear of the LORD.
> His delight shall be in the fear of the LORD.

We know that Isaiah was talking about Jesus when he said a shoot would come forth from the stump of Jesse; and the list of gifts from the verse are what we call the (seven) Gifts of the Spirit:

Piety (or reverence)
Fear of the Lord (or awe and wonder)
Knowledge, understanding and wisdom
Right judgement (or counsel)
Fortitude (or courage)

If you think about it, you can see how the first two gifts in this list help us to relate to God; and the remaining five help us to relate to our neighbour.

You have probably heard the story of the Pharisee who asked Jesus, 'Which is the greatest commandment of the Law?' Remember Jesus's reply – 'You must love the Lord your God with all your heart, with all your soul, and with all your mind. This is the greatest and the first commandment. The second resembles it: You must love your neighbour as yourself.'[39]

love the Lord your God with all your heart, with all your soul, and with all your mind

38 Isaiah 11:1-2
39 Matthew 22:36-40

Jesus was quoting from the Shema prayer said by devout Jews daily.[40]
The heart for the Jews is the centre of understanding, choosing and feeling; the mind the place of awareness; the soul the life energy of a person.

Jesus also quotes from another part of the law, the command to love one's neighbour as oneself.[41] This command is like the first, since the way we love ourselves and our neighbours is the way we express a genuine love for God.

These gifts of the Spirit help us to relate better to God:

the way we love ourselves and our neighbours is the way we express a genuine love for God

Piety (or reverence) helps us relate to God as a parent.

Fear of the Lord (or awe and wonder) is the gift that helps us to realise that God is beyond us; the word fear does not mean fear as such; it means awe.

And, these gifts help us personally and help us to help others:

Knowledge, understanding and wisdom will help us to see things as they are, will help us to know how to deal with our problems and difficulties and will help us to give advice to others.

Right judgement (or counsel) helps us to know what to do in the difficult situations of life.

Fortitude (or courage) gives us the ability to act on the truth as we see it even when there is a risk involved. It gives us the strength to do what we know is right – even when it is hard.

A task and some questions for discussion

Let's think about designing some people:

- a perfect brother or sister
- a perfect friend
- a perfect father or mother

How do you describe your perfect people? What characteristics do they have? What gifts do they have and how do they use them?

Did you describe a perfect friend or a brother or sister as someone who

- would be willing to listen when you're in trouble?
- would always be able to give you the right advice?
- would always be understanding?
- would defend you when someone misunderstands you or is upset by something you said – explaining what you really meant, explaining that you wouldn't have intended to upset them?

---

40 Deuteronomy 6:4-5.

41 Leviticus 19:18.

Did you describe a perfect mother or father as someone who

- you can rely on for help when you can't do your homework?
- who is always generous and kind?
- who is always understanding?
- who always knows just what to say when you are feeling down?

Can you see how many gifts of the Holy Spirit you've identified?

What message do we get?

The gifts of the Spirit are given to us – not just for us to keep – but for us to use for the benefit of others. As baptised people, we have been called to become like Jesus and to share in his work. Jesus was not a self-centered person; he was other-centered. How can we be like him?

The gifts of the Spirit are given to us – not just for us to keep – but for us to use for the benefit of others

We can begin by caring for our friends and family. We can help at home without being asked to. If we can play a musical instrument or we can sing, we can volunteer to join the music group at school or in the parish. If we are good at football, we might volunteer to coach primary school children. If we are thinking about being teachers, we might volunteer to help with First Communion preparation in the parish. We can include new students or new parishioners to join our activities. We can show our concern for the homeless by helping at a shelter or with a soup run. We can take environmental issues seriously by recycling. And we do something about all the poverty and illness in the world by raising funds for charities, which are devoted to helping.

We can make a difference to the world if we are willing to use the gifts we have for the benefit of others.

We can make a difference to the world

We pray

Spirit of the Living God,
Help us to notice the gifts you give us and to use them.
Help us to become more caring to one another,
help us to allow you to become more active in us.
We ask this through Christ, our Lord.
Amen.

Catechetical Sessions

SESSION 5

The Sacraments

We begin the session with a prayer.

The aims of this session are:

- to see how we encounter Christ in the sacraments; and
- to see that Confirmation confirms and strengthens what happened in baptism – and that, when you are confirmed, you say for yourself that you are followers of Christ.

Looking at our life experience

Our lives are full of symbolism – and much of it tells us we are loved.

WHEN my godmother celebrated her 80th birthday, I could not be with her. She lives in Florida and I live in London. I sent her flowers – which were, for her, a sign of my love. The flowers made me present for her; she experienced my love in a form which was visible.

Think of a time when someone's actions tell us something they feel about us.

God reveals his love through the sacraments

God loves us, cares for us, looks after us

God reveals his love and care for us through our world. Even though we don't always appreciate it, we are surrounded by things that tell us that God loves us, cares for us, looks after us. God is always searching for us, looking to have a relationship with us. One way God is revealed to us is in the world around us –

- in the beauty of nature – the sky, the sun, the sea
- in the majesty of nature – the trees, the mountains
- in the promise of nature – in the rising and setting of the sun

Another way God reveals his love and care for us is through people –

- through your parents and grandparents
- through your neighbours and
- through your friends

God is revealed through Jesus

The most important way in which God is revealed is through Jesus. The actions of Jesus always tell us that God loves us; they are symbolic actions. We believe that it is through the sacraments that Christ makes the love of God visible in our world. However, it is only when a person's love is manifested in a way I can understand that it becomes possible for me to enter into this love and I become personally confronted with this love for me. Edward Schillebeeckx explains this by giving an example like the one I used about giving my godmother flowers for her 80th birthday. The flowers were for her the concrete presence of my love: love in a form which is visible. He says that this is the case in the sacraments too because the proof Christ gives of his love is not turned into a lifeless thing. It is not merely an indication of something absent that somehow becomes present.[42]

encounters with God in Jesus take place in our world in the sacraments

In the sacraments, Jesus tells us that:

- He wants us to have new life in him in Baptism
- He wants us to be more like him and he strengthens us and confirms what happens in our baptism in confirmation
- He tells us that God always loves us – even when we fail in reconciliation
- He nourishes us with himself in the Eucharist
- He wants to heal us in the anointing of the sick
- Marriage is a life-giving relationship which reflects God's love for us
- He ordains priests to mediate between us and God

Signs are mere pointers to something... Symbols bring us into touch with realities, which are both familiar and mysterious

There are signs and symbols in all the sacraments.

Signs are mere pointers to something; they are an explanation of something. Symbols, on the other hand, point to something happening. Symbols bring us into touch with realities, which are both familiar and mysterious. For example, the love between a man and his wife is familiar; it is present to them day in and day out and, yet, it remains a mystery.

You will experience some signs and symbols in the sacrament of confirmation:

- the laying on of hands
- anointing with the oil of chrism
- signing with the cross
- the words, 'Be sealed with the Holy Spirit' to which you reply, 'Amen'.

You experienced two of these signs and symbols at your baptism:[43]

- you were anointed with the oil of chrism and
- you were signed with the cross.

---

42 Edward Schillebeeckx, *Christ the Encounter with God*, Sheed & Ward, London, 1966, pp 78-79.

43 You experienced other signs and symbols then too:
- you were anointed with the oil of catechumens
- water was poured over you as the priest or deacon said the words, 'I baptise you in the name of the Father, and of the Son and of the Holy Spirit'
- you were clothed in a white garment and
- you were given a baptismal candle.

when you were baptised you were called to share in the work of Jesus

Just before you were marked with the sign of the cross at your Baptism, the priest or deacon said, 'I claim you for Christ by the sign of his cross.' You were marked as a Christian – as a follower of Christ. The name Christ means 'the anointed one' and when you were baptised or Christ-ened (made like Christ) you were called to share in the work of Jesus, who came to us as priest, prophet and king.

A priest is someone whose work is to lead people to God by proclaiming God's word. A prophet (is not only someone who foretells the future, but) is someone who tells others the way God wants us to live. In the Bible, the word 'shepherd' was sometimes used as a title for the king. Jesus is our shepherd-king, who guides us, encourages us, feeds us, heals us and strengthens us as we journey to God's kingdom. And, as baptised people, we are invited to be priest, prophet and king. As baptised people, we are told – to the best of our ability – to carry on the mission of the whole Christian people in the Church and in the world.[44]

Confirmation confirms and strengthens what happened in baptism

Most of us were baptised as infants or small children. Someone else – our parents and our godparents – accepted this invitation for us. Confirmation confirms and strengthens what happened in baptism – so, when you are confirmed, you are saying that you accept this invitation for yourself.

Some questions for discussion

- Have you learned anything about baptism? and about confirmation?
- Do you think it is important to be baptised? to be confirmed?
- Can you see the link between baptism and confirmation?

Let us pray

with a Scripture meditation on the story of the baptism of Jesus. Begin by relaxing and being aware of how you are feeling and all the noises around us, all the people around us. Imagine that you are in Israel. We are walking along a dusty road towards the River Jordan. It's been a long walk and you are tired and thirsty. You can hear some noise in the distance. Is it the river? Can you hear people in the river? Gently climb down the banks of the river and notice what is happening. See and hear everything.

> There was this man called Jesus, who came from Nazareth of Galilee.
> He was being baptised by John in the Jordan.
> And just as he was coming up out of the water,
> the heavens tore apart and the Spirit descended like a dove on him.
> And a voice came from heaven.
> "You are my Son, the Beloved; with you I am well pleased."[45]

44 *Vatican II, Lumen Gentium, Dogmatic Constitution on the Church*, November 21, 1965, ¶31.
45 Mark 1:9-11 adapted.

Listen again to the words of the scripture. In the waters of the Jordan, something had happened. Imagine what it would have been like. Were you very hot? Go into the water with Jesus. What was it like? Were you near by? Could you see him well? Could you see the Spirit? Was it a dove? Did you hear the voice from heaven? Now, come out of the water and sit on the bank near Jesus. Talk to him and tell him what it was like for you to be there with him.

What message do we get?

As Jesus came up from the water, *"...the Spirit descended..."* Jesus was growing in awareness of his identity and his mission. What a moment that must have been for him. Hearing those words, Jesus undoubtedly would have been gripped by the full impact of his call to live out the role and mission of the servant.

For you, too, this sacrament of confirmation is the final step in your initiation into your identity as a follower of Christ and your mission. What an experience this is for you as you contemplate the full impact of your call to live out the role and mission of a servant to others.

Confirmation is the final step in your initiation

Blessing at the end of the session –

May God bless you and keep you as you prepare
to confirm and strengthen what happened at your baptism.
May God send you the Holy Spirit
making you courageous followers
of Jesus Christ, our Lord. Amen.

Catechetical Sessions

SESSION 6 Healed in Christ

We begin the session with a prayer.

The aims of this session are:

- to help to listen to Jesus, who tells us that God is always willing to have us be part of his family – even when we fail.
- to see how we are invited to celebrate the Sacrament of Reconciliation.

Looking at our life experience

Have you ever had to ask forgiveness of someone – knowing that they would never refuse to forgive you?

WHEN my son was small, I was working full-time and we had a nanny living with us to look after him. When he was about 3 years old, his nanny went out one day and bought some scarlet red nail varnish and painted her finger and toenails. My son was obviously fascinated by this; and, the next morning while the nanny and I were busy doing something, he went to her cupboard and found the nail varnish.
The scent of it reached me in the next room; I was able to find out where he was because there was a trail of scarlet red nail varnish – from the cupboard into my room and across the bottom of my bed. The trail ended on the beanbag in my bay window where my large and very elegant dog was lying. His paws were spread out and, you guessed it, his toenails were painted scarlet red! I was furious at my son; and I was furious at the dog! What self-respecting dog would sit there and let a 3-year old paint his nails? My son had no idea why I was so furious; after all, he was proud of his accomplishment! However, when he saw how upset I was, he said 'sorry'. He knew to do that even though he did not understand why he should be sorry. Naturally, I forgave him.

I forgave him. What else could I do?

Think of a time when you experienced forgiveness of this kind.

Let's listen to a story Jesus told about forgiveness –

The story of the prodigal son

"A man had two sons. The younger said to his father, 'Father, let me have the share of the estate that would come to me.' So the father divided the property between them. A few days later, the younger son got together everything he had and left for a distant country where he squandered his money on a life of debauchery.

"When he had spent it all, that country experienced a severe famine, and now he began to feel the pinch, so he hired himself out to one of the local inhabitants who put him on the farm to feed the pigs. And he would willingly have filled his belly with the husks the pigs were eating but no one offered him anything. Then he came to his senses and said 'How many of my father's paid servants have more food than they want, and here am I dying of hunger! I will leave this place and go to my father and say: Father, I have sinned against heaven and against you; I no longer deserve to be called your son; treat me as one of your paid servants.' So he left the place and went back to his father.

"While he was still a long way off, his father saw him and was moved with pity. He ran to the boy, clasped him in his arms and kissed him tenderly. Then his son said, 'Father, I have sinned against heaven and against you. I no longer deserve to be called your son.' But the father said to his servants 'Quick! Bring out the best robe and put it on him; put a ring on his finger and sandals on his feet. Bring the calf we have been fattening, and kill it; we are going to have a feast, a celebration, because this son of mine was dead and has come back to life; he was lost and is found.' And they began to celebrate.

"Now the elder son was out in the fields, and on his way back, as he drew near the house, he could hear music and dancing. Calling one of the servants, he asked what it was all about. 'Your brother has come,' replied the servant, 'and your father has killed the calf we had fattened because he has got him back safe and sound.' He was angry then and refused to go in, and his father came out to plead with him, but he answered his father, 'Look, all these years, I have slaved for you and never once disobeyed your orders, yet you never offered so much as a kid for me to celebrate with my friends. But, for this son of yours, when he comes back after swallowing up your property – he and his women – you kill the calf we had been fattening.'

"The father said, 'My son, you are with me always and all I have is yours. But it was only right we should celebrate and rejoice, because your brother here was dead and has come to life, he was lost and is found.' "[46]

46 Luke l5:11-32.

he was trying to tell them what God is like

This story was told to the Pharisees and the scribes when they complained. "This man", they said, "welcomes sinners and eats with them."[47] Note the context. They were complaining that Jesus's behaviour was unacceptable and offensive; he ate with tax collectors and sinners. It seems like he is telling this story to justify himself. But, I wonder if that was the only reason for telling it. I think he was really trying to tell them what God is like.

Now, remember how the story began, "A man has two sons, and the younger son says to his father, 'Father give me my share of the inheritance now!" What is your reaction? When do you get your inheritance?... You get it when your Father is dead! In effect, the boy is telling his father that he wishes he were dead! I can't wait any longer; I want my money now!

The story goes on, "So the father divided the property between them." As far as we hear in this story, the father does not argue with his son; he just gives him his share of the inheritance.

"A few days later, the younger son got together everything he had and left for a distant country." Note, he doesn't just pack a few things; he packs everything he had and leaves. There was not much chance for any contact; there was no postal system in those days – never mind mobile phones – to keep in touch.

In this far and distant land then, the story tells us that "he squandered his money on a life of debauchery" – which means sex, drink and riotous living. He spends all his money; and then, as if it wasn't bad enough, there is a severe famine in the country and he is left in a totally helpless situation. Notice Jesus's dramatic technique: he paints a picture that gets worse and worse.

What does the boy do? He is so desperate that he gets a job feeding pigs. You know what Jews are like with pork – they don't touch it. The boy is starving; the story says "he would willingly have filled his belly with the husks the pigs were eating but no one offered him anything". He has really hit the bottom of the barrel. And then, he remembers what his father is like. He remembers that, on his father's farm, even the "paid servants have more food than they want". So he decides to go back to his father and say, "Father, I have sinned against heaven and against you; I no longer deserve to be called your son; treat me as one of your paid servants."

Notice the boy does not think about how much he must have hurt his father by leaving, by asking for his inheritance before his father was dead. He is not terribly sorry about what he did; he is terribly hungry! He goes back for himself. He prepares a speech; he'll have to say something! He can't say he's come back because he is totally fed up and he is hungry. But, the important point is that he turns around and goes back.

The story goes on, giving us the impression that the father was looking out over the countryside. Perhaps he was hoping day after day that he would one day see his son coming home. If he was, he would have been thrilled this day to see him in the distance. He can't wait for him to reach the house; he takes

---

47 Luke 15:1-2.

the initiative and he rushes out to meet his son. He doesn't ask where the money has gone; he doesn't say, "Don't think you are coming back into this house!" We read that "he clasped him in his arms and kissed him tenderly." The father tells the servants to dress his son with the best robe and a ring for his finger and shoes for his feet. He has been accepted back into the family.

But the story goes on. When the older son returns from working in the fields and discovers that his brother has come home and that his father 'has killed the calf we had fattened because he has got him back safe and sound." The older brother was angry and refused to go into the party. Once again, the father takes the initiative – this time with the older son. He leaves the party to plead with him to come in. We have the impression that the relationship between the father and the older son was not good from the way he says to his father, 'all these years I have slaved for you and never once disobeyed your orders, yet you never offered so much as a kid for me to celebrate with my friends.' It doesn't give us the impression that the older son was working on the farm out of love for the father.

"he clasped him in his arms and kissed him tenderly."

Jesus was telling this story to tell people what God's love is like; unlike human love, God's love is unconditional; it is not a question of whether or not we deserve it. In this story, both sons got it wrong. The younger son thought he didn't deserve his father's love any more; the older son thought he should have his father's love because he did deserve it. God's love doesn't work that way.

God's love is unconditional

Questions for reflection/discussion

- What do you think it was like for the son to be forgiven?
- If you were the older son, would you have gone into the party?
- Do you see any similarity between the father and God?

What message do we get?

Just as this father gives his forgiveness, God invites us to do the same – to reflect the goodness and generosity of God to other people. I believe that Jesus is saying that, through the sacrament of reconciliation, I am giving you everything that the younger son received in the story.

Indeed, the story reminds us of the sacrament of reconciliation. Like the younger son remembering what his father is like, we remember what God is like and we go to him; like the son, we accept the forgiveness God is always willing to offer us. And, we celebrate the certainty of God's love in the sacrament.

A meditation on Rembrandt's painting of the return of the prodigal son

Just before he died, Rembrandt painted 'the Return of the Prodigal Son'. They say it is probably one of the last paintings he did. Rembrandt had suffered a lot through the loss of his wife and his only son; some say that this painting is an expression of his strong faith in the love of God. Have a look at a bit of the painting in black and white shown here; but if possible, have a copy of the picture in colour. Then, you can see how Rembrandt uses colour and light to show us how the son has moved from the darkness of his terrible experiences into the light of the love of his father. Rembrandt portrays the father as God – a God who does not wait to see what we have to say for ourselves; but who comes rushing out to meet us, who hugs us so closely that we can hardly see where the father ends and the son begins.

The son looks like so many of the homeless people we see today all over the world; his clothing is torn, his head is shaven, he is bruised and his shoes are hanging off his worn feet.

Can you see the expression on the father's face? You can see the tenderness in his eyes. Do you think he ever doubted that his son would return? Can you imagine how he must have wanted to have his son back?

Notice the father's hands; they are not a pair! One of the hands – the one on the left – is a man's hand, masculine and rough looking, it looks broad and strong. The other hand – the one on the right – looks more like a woman's hand, tender and fine. Some say that Rembrandt was saying that God is both father and mother to us.

Imagine the older son standing by and seeing this scene. Can you understand how he felt? Have you ever felt like that? You have obeyed the rules, been reliable and trustworthy and had all your efforts taken for granted. Perhaps you have found it hard to get excited when someone who has broken all the rules, who has been unreliable and could never be trusted finally does something right and they are celebrated for that one single thing they have done.

And, we finish our meditation

by resting for a moment in this scene – knowing that there are times when we are like the younger son and there are times when we are like the older son.

> Gracious and loving God, help us to be more like the father in this story,
> more like you – reflecting your goodness and generosity to people.
> We ask this through Christ, our Lord. Amen.

Catechetical Sessions

The Ten Commandments

We begin the session with a prayer.

The aims of this session are:

- to look at the Ten Commandments in a way that is relevant to our lives today.
- to see that the Ten Commandments challenge us to think about being a follower of Christ – and the difference that makes in the choices we make in our lives.

Looking at our life experience

Imagine the caption of this cartoon.

AS MOSES comes down from Mount Sinai with the Ten Commandments, the men at the foot of the mountain are saying to one another, "Don't you think it would be better to call them recommendations or suggestions rather than commandments?"

Think of how you react when you are told what to do or what not to do. I know that I am far more likely to do what I am told when I am given a recommendation or a suggestion than when I am given an order – a commandment.

What about you? Can you identify with what I am saying?

God gave us the Commandments

We often take so many words to say what we mean. A Jewish lawyer approached Jesus wanting to know what exactly was his message. "Which commandment is the first of all?" he asked. He didn't want a long explanation. Jesus replied" 'You shall love the Lord your God with all your heart, and with all your soul, and with all your mind.' This is the greatest and first commandment. And a second is like it: 'You shall love your neighbour as yourself.' "[48]

"Which commandment is the first of all?"

Do we really understand what Jesus meant? Mark even adds something more. In his version of this same story, he says that Jesus said we must "love the Lord your God with all your heart, with all your soul, with all your mind and with all your strength."[49] There is no escape clause here! Jesus was talking about a passionate love of God and of others with no half measures.

"love the Lord Your God with all your heart, with all your soul, with all your mind and with all your strength."

People often think of the commandments as a set of rather tiresome rules which they must obey in to avoid offending God – and, if we manage to obey them, that we will be rewarded. But, God doesn't love us because we are good; he loves us because he is good.

Remember how we reflected on the goodness and generosity of God in our last session. By loving our neighbour as ourself – with that same goodness and generosity – we come to know and love God. This is because it is only through our experiences of love in this world that we can experience the love of God.

You might use the set of questions on the following pages as the basis of group discussions on what the Ten Commandments mean today – how they can help us to understand more about this passionate love Jesus was talking about.

God doesn't love us because we are good; he loves us because he is good

The Ten Commandments and some questions for group discussion

1. I am the Lord your God; you shall not have strange Gods before me.

What comes first in your life? Is it God or is it you?
Do your possessions come before the people around you?

2. You shall not take the name of the Lord your God in vain.

Do you say things like, For God's sake!
The more you use the word God, the less it may mean.

3. Remember to keep the Lord's day holy.

Is Sunday any different from other days?
Do you rest on Sundays?
Is it important to you to go to Mass on Sundays?

48 Matthew 22:36-39.
49 Mark 12:29-31.

4. Honour your father and your mother.

Do you treat your parents with respect?
Do you appreciate their love and concern?
Do you tell your parents the truth?

5. You shall not kill.

What do you think about violence?
Are you in favour of nuclear weaponry and war?
Do you think abortion is right? What about euthanasia?
Do you think it is OK to use drugs?
And, do you think it is OK to smoke cigarettes (despite the health warning on each pack)?

6. You shall not commit adultery.

What do you think about marriage?
Do you think married people should be faithful to one another?
Do you think sex is something special, sacred in marriage?

7. You shall not steal.

Do you take what does not belong to you?
Do you waste time?
Do you cheat people, or cheat on tests at school?
Do you respect what does not belong to you?

8. You shall not tell lies against your neighbour.

How important is this Commandment to you?
Do you tell the truth to people? Do you tell the truth about people?
Do you gossip? Do you listen to gossip? Do you exaggerate?
So much damage can be caused by gossip.
What do you do when you hear it?

9. You shall not want to take your neighbour's wife or husband.

Do you treat your friends like possessions?
Are you jealous or envious of the friendships of others?
Do you respect the friendships of your friends?

10. You shall not want to take your neighbour's possessions.

Are you happy with what you have? Or do you want what others have?
Are you jealous of the opportunities others are given?

What message do we get?

If we say that we want to be followers of Christ, it will make a difference to the choices we make in our lives

If we say that we want to be followers of Christ, it will make a difference to the choices we make in our lives. We will ask, 'What would Jesus do?' or 'What would Jesus say?' when we are faced with the choices we have to make.

Let us pray

Gracious and loving God,
help us to love our neighbour as ourselves
and help us to love you in all that we say and do.
We ask this through Christ, our Lord. Amen.

Catechetical Sessions

SESSION 8

The Beatitudes

We begin the session with a prayer.

The aims of this session are:

- to see that, as a follower of Christ, our every action and attitude is inspired by the life and the person of Jesus Christ.

Looking at our life experience

I HEARD a story about a man who worked late in the City one evening. Tired by the long day's work, he bought a newspaper and got on the tube to go home. The tube was nearly empty and he sat down to read the paper in peace. At the next station, a father with two children came into his carriage. The father sat quietly while his children ran up and down disturbing everyone. When he could stand the noise and the irritation any longer, the man said to the father, "Are you aware that your children are disturbing everyone in this carriage?" The father replied, "You see, we have just come from the hospital where their mother has died and they don't know how to react." The man changed his attitude immediately. He was no longer irritated; his heart went out in sympathy for this father and his children.

Nothing changed but his attitude. Have you ever had such a shift in your attitude – seeing things from a completely different perspective?

The beatitudes are at the heart of Jesus's preaching [50]

To genuinely encounter Christ is to have one's life turned upside down and inside out! Paradoxically, Jesus promises happiness and joy to those who experience poverty, hunger, grief, abuse and rejection. This is what he did in the sermon on the mount. Listen to the way Matthew tells the story:

Paradoxically, Jesus promises happiness and joy to those who experience poverty, hunger, grief, abuse and rejection

50 *The Catechism*, ¶1716

"Seeing the crowds, he went onto the mountain. And when he was seated, his disciples came to him. Then he began to speak. This is what he taught them:

'How blessed are the poor in spirit: the kingdom of Heaven is theirs.
Blessed are the gentle; they shall have the earth as their inheritance.
Blessed are those who mourn; they shall be comforted.
Blessed are those who hunger and thirst for uprightness;
they shall have their fill.
Blessed are the merciful; they shall have mercy shown them.
Blessed are the pure in heart; they shall see God.
Blessed are the peacemakers; they shall be recognised as children of God.
Blessed are those who are persecuted in the cause of uprightness;
the kingdom of Heaven is theirs.' "[51]

The Commandments deal with our actions. They tell us right from wrong. The Beatitudes go deeper; they deal with our attitudes. They go to the heart of our Christian belief. The right attitude is what is important. In order to be fully human, we must

be kind	**be generous**	**be honest**
be loving	**be peaceful**	**be pure in heart**

we all know that beatitudes means blessed; but let's look at them as these "be-attitudes"

Now, we all know that beatitudes means blessed; but for the purpose of understanding what Jesus was trying to say to us, let's look at them as these "be-attitudes". These are the kinds of attitude we should have. We want a comfortable life-style; we want our material possessions and we don't always notice the high price we pay. Often, when we are busy accumulating these material possessions (or protecting them when we've got them), we are not relying on God. That's what the beatitudes are really about. Let's spend some time talking about them.

Blessed are the poor in spirit theirs is the kingdom of heaven.

What is Jesus trying to say? It certainly seems strange to say that the poor are lucky! Jesus was saying that nothing stands between the poor and God; they can admit that they have needs, they are open to change. They realise that they don't have it all.

Blessed are the meek for they shall inherit the earth.

Here is a similar riddle to the first beatitude. It seems to be saying that you are lucky if you are not important. Those who enable others to be themselves, to listen, to be quiet enough to hear others – they are the lucky ones. God has created every one of us and He loves us all equally. Do we know that, truly know it? Does the way we act reflect the fact that we know it?

51 Matthew 5:1-12.

Blessed are they that mourn, for they shall be comforted.

We all crave for love and affection, for reassurance. We have certain things in common with each other: we all get hurt, we all lack in confidence, we all want to be loved – especially by those we love. Although we are all the same, we do not remember that others feel as much in need of help and love as we are. Sometimes we are not sensitive to the hardships of others. But, we are lucky when our experiences of being hurt help us to feel the pain of others.

Blessed are they that hunger and thirst after justice; they shall be satisfied.

We have certain things in common with each other: we all want to be loved – especially by those we love.

The world has enough for everyone in it; yet we don't share equally the world's resources. We have so much; do we think about how we can share it with others? We taste the need for justice when we ourselves have been treated unjustly. What do we do about the injustices around us that affect others? Those who are hungry to see that others are treated justly are the ones who are lucky. They are doing God's will.

Blessed are the merciful; they shall obtain mercy.

How do we see God? Do you see him as forgiving, merciful and gentle? Do we realise that we are ourselves in need of forgiveness and mercy? Accepting God's love is what it is all about. The more we accept it, the more it becomes ours. The more we experience God's forgiveness, the more we can experience it by being forgiving to ourselves and to others.

Blessed are the pure of heart; they shall see God.

God is straight with us; he is honest and fair; he is truthful. Those who are like that get close to God. How lucky they are!

Blessed are the peacemakers for they shall be called children of God.

How lucky we are when we can make friends with people – not just people who are like us, but those who are a different colour, a different race, a different age, a different religion. It is sometimes hard to understand those who are different; it is easy to reject those who have a different opinion from ours. How lucky we are when we learn to accept others as we want them to accept us.

how lucky we are when we accept others as we want them to accept us

Blessed are they that suffer persecution for justice's sake; theirs is the kingdom of heaven.

Do we admire people who are persecuted because they stand for justice, for what is right? There are so many people who are willing to stand up for what they believe is right; many of them, even today, are persecuted. How many times have you been a coward, have you been afraid to speak out for what you believe in, to defend someone who is being unjustly accused – for fear of getting in trouble yourself?

What message do we get?

The Beatitudes are far from vague! The Jesus we meet in the Gospels is someone who ate with sinners and outcasts; he defended the poor and unimportant. He pitied the broken-hearted; he was compassionate to those who suffered. He stood up for what he believed was right; but he was not aggressive about it. He was gentle with those he met and he was honest with people and he invites us to do the same.

We pray

Gracious and loving God,
Give us hearts that are kind and understanding,
Take away our pride, our fear and our anger
and give us the kind of 'be-attitudes'
which will allow us to be kind,
to be generous, to be loving, be peaceful and to be pure in heart.
We ask this through Christ, our Lord. Amen.

Celebration 2

Mass of Commitment

The catechetical period has now come to an end. It has been a time of learning and you have been challenged to think about what it means to be a follower of Christ - and what difference that makes in your lives. If you want to continue with your preparation for confirmation, you are ready for the Mass of Commitment.

At this second celebration, the catechists will be asked if you understand the importance of what you are doing. They will be asked if you are willing to continue with your preparations to be confirmed. So that it is clear that this is your decision you, too, will be asked if you are willing to continue.

Your parents and the parish community will be asked if they are willing to continue to support and guide you by their prayers and example. By doing this, they are reminded of the responsibilities they have towards you.

You will now enter a more prayerful period as the date of their Confirmation approaches.

At the beginning of the Mass, the priest will probably want to welcome you in a special way. He will say something about the fact that today you are committing yourselves to continue in the parish programme for preparation for the sacrament of confirmation.

After the Gospel, the following questions will be asked. In some parishes, the questions are included in a Mass booklet which includes the readings of the day and hymns which will be sung at that Mass.[52]

Catechist	'Bishop N... will be celebrating the sacrament of confirmation here in our parish on [date]. I would like to present to the parish our young people who are preparing to celebrate the sacrament. [A list of the candidates is now read].' As each person's name is read out, they stand and remain standing. When all the names have been called out, the priest will ask them to sit.
The priest	asks the catechist: 'In the name of this community, you and the other catechists have been working to prepare these young people for the sacrament of confirmation. 'Do they understand the importance of what they are doing?' The catechist replies 'They do'. The priest asks 'Are they willing to continue to take part conscientiously in the preparation programme?' The catechist replies 'They are'.

52 You will find a simple booklet in the next section that you can use if you are not going to include the hymns and references to the readings in a booklet.

He addresses the candidates saying 'Do you agree to take part in the sessions and activities that are a part of this programme? Are you willing to open your minds and hearts to the activities of the Holy Spirit during this time of preparation? And, do you pray for a deeper growth in faith and hope and love?' They reply, 'We do'

He then asks the parents of the candidates and the parish community if they are willing to continue to support and pray for these young people as they continue to prepare for the sacrament of confirmation and they reply 'We are'.

He concludes by addressing the young people: 'May God bless you as you continue your preparations for the Sacrament of Confirmation.'

Final Preparation Sessions

The Creed

SESSION 9

We begin the session with a prayer.

The aims of this session are:

- to help us think about what we believe in. The Creed is our profession of faith – something we recite every Sunday when we come to Mass.
- to help prepare us to renew our baptismal promises when we are confirmed.

Looking at our life experience

LET'S think about things we believe in for a few minutes. One of my favourite songs is "I have a dream" sung by Abba. The words, at one point say, "I believe in angels – something good in everything I see".
I like the song because I believe in the power of dreams. I am not talking about the dreams we have when we sleep. I'm talking about the dreams we have for our future – our hopes, our aspirations for ourselves and for our friends and families.

Think about something you believe in. Perhaps, you believe in being loyal to your friends, perhaps, the way you treat your friends is important to you.

Now, let's look at the Apostles' Creed – our profession of faith

I believe in God the Father Almighty
creator of heaven and earth
and in Jesus Christ, his only Son, our Lord,
who was conceived by the Holy Spirit, born of the Virgin Mary,
suffered under Pontius Pilate, was crucified, died and was buried.
He descended into hell. The third day he rose again from the dead.

He ascended into heaven, sitteth at the right hand of
God the Almighty Father.
From thence he shall come to judge the living and the dead.
I believe in the Holy Spirit,
the Holy Catholic Church, the communion of saints,
the forgiveness of sins, the resurrection of the body
and life everlasting. Amen

From the beginning, Christians have tried to summarise their faith in short statements. For example, they used to say "Jesus is the Christ" or "Jesus is Lord" – Lord in a way that no one else is Lord, none of the gods revered by the nations, nor the Roman emperor. During the first centuries, in times of persecution, Christians went to their death as martyrs for this profession of faith.

We believe the Creed it is a summary of the Christian message handed down from the apostles.

The *Apostles' Creed* is the most usual profession of faith. It is called the Apostle's Creed because we believe it is a summary of the Christian message handed down from the apostles. In the very early days of Christianity, the three sections of this creed were answers to the three questions addressed to the catechumens at baptism:

- Do you believe in God, the almighty Father?
- Do you believe in Jesus Christ, our Saviour?
- Do you believe in the Holy Spirit and in his work?

You are asked to declare for yourselves what your parents and godparents declared for you at your baptism.

These same three questions are still asked when Christians renew their baptismal promises at the Easter Vigil. These same three questions will be asked of you at your confirmation when you are asked to declare for yourselves what your parents and godparents declared for you at your baptism.

This is the Profession of Faith you will be asked to make.
To each question, you will be asked to reply, "I do."

- Do you believe in God, the Father almighty, creator of heaven and earth?
- Do you believe in Jesus Christ, his only Son, our Lord, who was born of the Virgin Mary, was crucified, died and was buried, rose from the dead and is now seated at the right hand of the Father?
- Do you believe in the Holy Spirit, the holy catholic Church, the communion of saints, the forgiveness of sins, the resurrection of the body and the life everlasting?

We recite these beliefs in the Creed every Sunday when we go to Mass; but what do we think of when we say "I believe in God"?

Who is God for you?

- Do you think about going to church?
- Do you think about creation?
- Do you think about love?
- What do you think?
- Who is God for you?

When we say "I believe in Jesus Christ", what do we think of?

- Do you think about someone who knew everything?
  Did he know about computers when he was a baby in Nazareth?
- Do you think he is someone who shows us how to live?
- Do you think he knew everything that was going to happen during his lifetime on earth?
- Do you imagine him in long white robes or in jeans and a sweatshirt? How do you see him?
- Who is Jesus for you?

Who is Jesus for you?

When we say "I believe in the holy Catholic Church", what do we think of?

- the building? or
- all the people? or
- the pope, the cardinals, the bishops, the priests – the institution?

What or who is the Church for you?

A little story to help us see where we meet God

In the southern states of the United States, there are often storms and floods. People are evacuated from their homes sometimes; often electricity is cut when the storms are bad. On one such occasion, the storm came almost without warning, the police were going around warning people to leave their homes. There was a man who believed in God. He was praying that the storm would stop and he was confident God would protect him. And so, he refused to leave his house.

An hour later, the storm was getting worse. This time, a tank was sent into the area to get people to leave. The man was sitting in his living room looking out the window. Again, he refused to leave, saying "I believe in God; I am relying on him to protect me."

More time passed and the floods had risen to a depth of eight feet. The man was now upstairs in his bedroom. A rescue boat passed his house and asked him what on earth he was still doing there. He said he was not leaving the house; God was going to protect him. He would be OK.

Now the storm continued and the whole area was evacuated. The only one left was this man. The water had now reached the top of the house and he was sitting on the roof. A helicopter passed by and called down to him to catch hold of a rope so that they could rescue him. He refused again. A while later, he drowned.

When he got to heaven, he was mad! He met God and said to him, "I believed in you and you let me down. I waited and waited and I prayed and I prayed and you didn't save me." God looked at him patiently and said to him "I came to you in a car, I came to you in a tank, I came to you in a boat and I came to you in a helicopter; but you didn't recognise me!"

Author unknown

And, now an imaginative exercise to help us see Jesus today.

"Imagine a ring at your doorbell one evening and on answering, you discover the visitor is the Risen Lord himself. Somehow, you know it is the Lord. How do you react, what do you say? Do you shut the door on him, or tell him to come back on Sunday? Presumably, you welcome him in, summon everyone in the house, and find yourself making such ridiculous statements to the Lord of all creation as 'Do make yourself at home and stay as long as you like. Everything is yours.' Now take a fortnight's leap in your imagination. Jesus has accepted your invitation and he is still with you. How are things at home now? You remember that disturbing passage in the gospel where Jesus says, 'I have come not to bring peace, but the sword, to set daughter against mother, daughter-in-law against mother-in-law, son against father.' The letter to the Hebrews says 'Jesus Christ is the same today as he was yesterday and as he will be forever', so presumably there has been a bit of friction over family meals in the last two weeks, some members leaving the table, slamming doors, possibly the front door, never to return. You invited Jesus to make himself at home, so he has begun inviting his friends to your house. You remember what people said of his friends in the Gospel, how he dined with sinners. What kind of people do you see coming now to your house, what are the neighbours saying, and what is happening to the local property values? Then you decide that you must not keep Jesus all to yourself, so you arrange for him to give a talk at the local church. You remember that scene in the Gospel where he addresses the scribes, Pharisees and chief priests and assures them that the criminals and the prostitutes will get into the kingdom of God before they do. He gives the same message to a gathering of men and women at St. Jude's parish and there is uproar, the parish losing its principal benefactors.

You return home with Jesus, your Saviour, who has now become your problem. What are you to do? You cannot throw out the Lord of all creation. So you look around the house, find a suitable cupboard, clear it out, decorate it, sparing no expense, get a good strong lock on it and put Jesus inside. Outside you can have a lamp and flowers, and each time you pass, bow reverently, so that you now have Jesus and he does not interfere any more![53]

What do we believe?

Write your own creed now – either in a group or on your own; but write a statement of what you believe in. You might use some of what has been written at the Confirmation Mass in some way.

We pray

Gracious and loving God, we thank you for the light and life
you continually give us through others.
May we continue to discover new ways of recognising your light in our life
and never be afraid to let that light shine.
We ask this through your Son, Jesus Christ. Amen.

53 *Oh God, Why?* by Gerard W. Hughes, The Bible Reading Fellowship, Oxford, 1993, pp 23-24.

Final Preparation Sessions

The Mass

SESSION 10

We begin the session with a prayer.

The aims of this session are:

- to think about praying as part of our parish community (particularly at Mass) since it is into this community that we are initiated when we are confirmed.
- to help us think about what the Mass means to us

Looking at our life experience

ONE of my very special friends, Nancy, came from Atlanta, Georgia. She, like me, came to London and settled down. We were friends for about 20 years when she said she would have to go back to Atlanta to take care of her sick mother. It was a blow for us; Nancy had celebrated every Christmas, every birthday, every Easter with us for all those years. The first Christmas she was gone, we spent the whole time talking about what Nancy would have done if she had been there. Nancy would have brought eggnog – her special recipe from Georgia; she'd have brought music to play; she'd have brought some silly toy or game – something to make us laugh. We really felt her absence. Then, at the end of our lunch, the phone rang and it was Nancy! We put the phone, with its primitive speaker on the dining room table so that we could all talk to her. Suddenly, Nancy was present with us!

Think about a special occasion you have celebrated – a birthday, a wedding, an anniversary. Now think about someone special who was there – and they made the party. It wouldn't have been the same without them. Now think about someone who was ill and they could not come. Did it make a difference that they could not be there? Did you notice their absence?

Let's look at the Mass

We go to Mass because we belong to God's family – as members of Christ's Church. In the same way we notice someone in the family who is missing from a special celebration, we are missed if we do not go to Mass.

This is particularly important today – in a world where we so much need to know we belong, in a world where so many things undermine the sense of belonging we need for our well-being. It is a world where family break-up, unemployment, redundancy, closure of hospitals, phasing out of smaller schools and changes in religious practice are the norm – were so many people feel on the outside, feel rejected.

Jesus speaks again and again to us of those who are on the outside – the rejects of society – as those who belong to him. This is good news!
It is reassuring. The problem is that is hard is to believe it and accept it.

If we want to have this kind of faith, we need to belong to a community of others who believe it, people who support each other in practical ways as well as sharing prayer and thanking God for what they have, for who they are.

In our Mass, we find a community where all are welcome, where all are needed.

To understand the Mass better, let's reflect on the life of Jesus and see how the steps in his life are mirrored in the themes of the Mass [54]

Raymond Topley talks about, what he calls, the five steps in the life of Jesus. Let's look at them in order to help us to understand the Eucharist better. When Jesus began his public ministry, one of the first things he did was to call people to follow him. He said, "Come follow me."[55] Jesus formed a community; and we believe that it is as members of a community that we come to know God through Jesus. Likewise, in the first part of the Mass, we come together; we gather as a community – believing that where "two or three are gathered in his name"[56] Jesus is in the midst of us.[57]

When people came, Jesus said "Listen to me, all of you, and understand."[58] Jesus taught them the secret of his life – the story of his relationship with God, whom he called Father. He told his followers that the good news is that they, too, are part of that relationship. In the same way, in the Mass, we have the Liturgy of the Word, where we listen to Scripture.

We believe that, in Scripture, God speaks to us. The writers of the Old Testament and the New Testament used stories, statements, songs and letters to pass on God's message about how they understood God, how they experienced God, how they related to God and how God related to them. This is

54 Raymond Topley (Maynooth) wrote about this in 1990 in a booklet called *The Eucharist*.

55 Mark 1:18.

56 Matthew 18:20.

57 We believe that Jesus is "really present" in the gathering, *Sacrosanctum Concilium, Vatican II, The Constitution on the Sacred Liturgy*, December 1963, ¶7.

58 Mark 7:15.

how we come to know another person - by spending time with them, really spending time with them. We have to listen to them, to speak with them, share experiences with them, to relate to them and let them relate to us. It is no different with God. God is revealed to us in Scripture, we come to recognise God in our lives, to come to know the person of Jesus. When we listen to the Scripture at Mass, we believe that Jesus is "really present"[59] - just as present as he was when he walked the roads of Galilee.

The followers of Jesus noticed that he prayed a good deal. His prayer was often one of giving thanks. Whenever he took and broke bread, he gave thanks - "Thanks he gave to God."[60] The central action of the Mass is that of giving thanks. In fact, Eucharist means thanksgiving. In the Eucharistic prayer, we thank God, our father, for sending us his Son, Jesus, as our saviour; and we remember that Jesus has died for us and that he was raised to life by the Father.

At the last supper, Jesus asked his disciples to continue to do what he did in memory of him. He said, "Take and eat. This is my body."[61] In the Mass, through the action of the Holy Spirit, the bread and wine are changed into the body and blood of Christ. Here, we believe that Christ is "really present"[62] in a unique way. At communion, we take and eat. We are joined to Christ and are nourished by him—becoming more and more the Body of Christ.

The last command of Jesus before he ascended to his father was "Go out to the whole world, tell them the good news and baptise."[63] This is called the missionary mandate of Jesus. In just the same way, the last thing that the priest says to us at the end of the Mass is "Go in peace to love and serve the Lord." This is our missionary mandate; and, each time we go to Mass, each time we receive the eucharist, Jesus is sending us out to be more and more like him, to follow him - living in such a way as to make the world a better place for others.

There is one other thing to think about when we reflect on the life of Jesus and on the Mass. Throughout Jesus's life, we hear about forgiveness over and over again. It is also a theme that runs through the Mass:

- We begin the Mass by forgiving one another and asking forgiveness of God and of one another.
- When we say the Our Father, we ask God to forgive us as we forgive others.
- When we share the sign of peace, we show that we want to be friends with those around us and that we are wishing them peace.

59 *Sacrosanctum Concilium*, December 1963, ¶7.

60 Matthew 14:19.

61 Matthew 26:26.

62 *Sacrosanctum Concilium*, December 1963, ¶7.

63 Mark 16:15 and Matthew 28:19.

For discussion, what does the Mass mean to you?

- Do you feel welcome in the Church?
- Do you see the point of gathering together?
- Do you feel you meet Jesus in the Mass?
- Do you see why Confirmation is celebrated at a Mass?
- Do you realise you are bringing your gifts? the gift of yourself?

We pray

Jesus, as we lift our hands to receive you in the Eucharist,
Help us to recognise you and welcome you.
Expand our hearts that we might understand that we are saying
'yes' to you,
'yes, I want to follow you' – opening our hearts to others,
sharing what we have and serving them with the gifts you have given us
and 'yes, I want to be more like you'. Amen.

A day of recollection

Here are some notes of a day of recollection you might find useful

These are the notes from a day of recollection with a group of candidates preparing to be confirmed. Use it as it is if you think it will work well with your group; and adapt it to make it your own. Once again, I have included my stories in Session 1. I warn you, though, this time it will not work using my stories; for the day to work, the catechists must tell their own stories!

Try to find a venue for the day which is comfortable and welcoming. Ideally, it should have somewhere pleasant outside for the candidates to go during the breaks and during the lunchtime. There should be one catechist for each 6 candidates if possible. You will need a large hall where the group can meet as a group in the centre – with cluster groups around the edge of the room. (If this is not possible, you can have a large room where the whole group meets and small rooms for the cluster groups to go to.)

The proposed timetable:

10:00 – 10:30 am	Arrivals – welcome, gathering and a drink
10:30 – 11:30 am	Session 1: *On our call* – a series of three scripture reflections and discussions introduced by the lead catechist. Gather to hear the first reading and a brief input; then break into the established groups, each led by a catechist, who will share something to start and then invite others to talk
11:30 – 12:00 pm	Break
12:00 – 1:00 pm	Session 2: *Take a stand!* – the choices we make as Christians (based on the Ten Commandments)
1:00 – 2:00 pm	Lunch
2:00 – 3:00 pm	Session 3: *Liturgy preparation in five groups* • *Readers* – some candidates to consider dramatising or miming one of the readings. Readings of the day to be used if possible. • *Music* – some candidates to prepare the music • *Bidding prayers* – some candidates to write up bidding prayers (considering, perhaps, presenting a votive candle when each is prayed) • *Offertory* – some candidates to make pictures or sculptures to represent the gifts they have and want to offer to God and to their community • *Venue* – some candidates to organise the place where Mass will be celebrated.
3:00 – 4:00 pm	Mass
4:00 pm	Finish

Session 1 **On our Call**

First reflection

Based on Jeremiah 1:4-10

> "Now the word of the LORD came to me saying,
> "Before I formed you in the womb I knew you,
> and before you were born I consecrated you;
> I appointed you a prophet to the nations."
> Then I said, "Ah, Lord GOD! Truly I do not know how to speak,
> for I am only a boy."
> But the LORD said to me, "Do not say, 'I am only a boy';
> for you shall go to all to whom I send you,
> and you shall speak whatever I command you,
> Do not be afraid of them, for I am with you to deliver you, says the LORD."
> Then the LORD put out his hand and touched my mouth;
> and the LORD said to me, "Now I have put my words in your mouth.
> See, today I appoint you over nations and over kingdoms, to pluck up
> and to pull down, to destroy and to overthrow, to build and to plant."

Input:

Jeremiah lived in a village near Jerusalem. He was still very young when God called him and said: "I have chosen you... to be a prophet to the nations."
His first reaction to God was, "What, me?! I am too young; nobody will listen to me – I won't know what to say."

Personal story of the catechist – at that first call

I FELT like Jeremiah when I first realised that God was calling me, when my parish priest asked me to help with the Confirmation programme in my parish. Why me? Surely, there were plenty of people who were far more suitable than I was. I was working in the City as a manager in a law firm. I was not religious; the very prospect of being a catechist was ridiculous, I thought. I had been away from the Church for 20 years.
I hadn't even dared to tell my colleagues at work that I was a Catholic or that I had started to go to church again. How could I be a catechist? I didn't know enough anyway. What would I say to a group of teenagers? And, if people in the parish knew about me and knew that I'd been away from the Church for a long time, surely, they wouldn't listen to me, would they?

Questions for discussion

- Have you ever found yourself in a situation where you were afraid to say what you believe in?
- Have you ever felt you didn't know enough, couldn't speak well enough, that no-one would listen to you even though you thought you had something important to say?

Second reflection

Based on Matthew 4:18-22

> "As he walked by the Sea of Galilee, he saw two brothers,
> Simon, who is called Peter, and Andrew his brother,
> casting a net into the sea – for they were fishermen.
> And he said to them, "Follow me, and I will make you fish for people."
> Immediately they left their nets and followed him.
> As he went from there, he saw two other brothers,
> James son of Zebedee and his brother John,
> in the boat with their father Zebedee, mending their nets, and he called them.
> Immediately they left the boat and their father, and followed him."

Input:

According to this story, Jesus is walking along and invites Simon and Andrew to follow him. Now, they may have heard of Jesus; but, even so, imagine just following him when he invites you! They were ordinary fishermen and were in the middle of doing their ordinary work. Imagine going to the supermarket and meeting Jesus there and imagine that he asks you to follow him. Would you?

As the story goes on, he went on a bit further and he saw two other brothers, James son of Zebedee and his brother John, in the boat with their father Zebedee, mending their nets, and he called them. Again, without any apparent question, they left the boat and their father, and followed him. Again, I ask you, if you were mowing the front lawn or mending the car with your father and Jesus walked past your house and asked you to follow him, would you? What do you think your father would say?

Personal story of the catechist at the time we agreed to follow Jesus

AFTER a couple of years of helping with the Confirmation group in the parish, I wanted to know more and I asked if there were any courses for catechists. I found being a catechist very fulfilling and I was really enthusiastic about it. I began to resent the long hours I was working in the City; I began to realise that there was more to life than working so hard and giving such long hours to my job – even though I was earning a lot of money. Then I went to

Africa one summer and I met some youngsters who were doing their laundry in the river. Their families had no money, they had no electricity and no running water in their homes.
They had no TV and no telephone. But, they were happy. These young boys helped me to realise I was unhappy. I left my job and I spent 4 years studying theology – using all the money I had to pay for my studies and to support myself while I was studying. Some of my friends thought I was doing the right thing; many thought I had gone a bit mad. But I knew that I was doing the right thing.

Questions for discussion

- Talk about some people you know who are called in some way.
- Consider what you might be called to do and how you will respond.

Third reflection

Based on Luke 10:1-6

> "After this the Lord appointed seventy others and sent them on ahead of him in pairs to every town and place where he himself intended to go.
> He said to them, "The harvest is plentiful, but the labourers are few; therefore ask the Lord of the harvest to send out labourers into his harvest.
> Go on your way. See, I am sending you out like lambs into the midst of wolves.
> Carry no purse, no bag, no sandals; and greet no one on the road.
> Whatever house you enter, first say, 'Peace to this house!'
> And if anyone is there who shares in peace, your peace will rest on that person; but if not, it will return to you."

Input:

Having spent some time with Jesus, he now sends his followers out to do something. He makes it sound very appealing, huh? Imagine what they must have felt like when he told them they would be like lambs in the midst of wolves, that should carry no purse, no bag; that they should greet no-one on the road.

Personal story of the catechist – on what it was like to be sent out

WHILE I was studying, I worked part-time in a couple of parishes – partly because I needed the money and partly because I wanted the experience. I was working closely with the priests in the parishes and I learned a lot from them. Once I finished studying, I began to work full-time. It was not easy! People expected me to know what to do, they expected me to know what to say and they expected me to have the answers to their questions. Some of the people I worked with didn't want to work with a lay

person; they wanted to work with the priest. Some of the men didn't want to work with a woman. Some would not listen to me; their image of God was so different from mine. I had been warned that it wouldn't be easy; but I did not think it would be as hard as it was.
There are just not enough catechists to do all the work there is to do; and it is hard to find more catechists. Worst of all, things are often very, very messy. These are not new problems; Jesus talked about how few labourers there were and I realised that it was pretty messy in his time too.
One thing I must say, though, is that in many ways the work is very fulfilling and rewarding. It is the work I want to do and I believe that it is what God wants me to do.

Questions for discussion

- Have you ever been asked to do something – and then you are told how awful it might be, what risks might be involved? How willing were you to go and do it?
- What do you think your life as a Christian will be like as you look to the future?

Session 2 **Take a Stand!**

The aim of this session is to allow the candidates time and space to think about the choices they make in life – time to consider how, as Christians, we choose to follow Christ. What effect does this have on the choices they make in life?

Put up a sign at one end of the room saying, "I AGREE" another at the other end of the room saying, "I DISAGREE" and a third sign in the middle of the room saying, "I DON'T KNOW". After each statement or question, people must go to one of the three places. They must be ready to defend their position at either end of the room; and, anyone (including the ones in the middle) can move at any time they change their minds (or make their minds up).
They must make up their own minds; not to follow the flock because they may be challenged as to why they are where they are! At the end of each debate, you might ask which commandment(s) apply.

The point of this debate is to give you a chance to talk through some of the issues you are facing or you might face in a *safe* environment. You are not being asked to be judgmental.

1. *What do you do?* You go into a shop and you buy some groceries for home. You go to the cash desk to pay; the bill comes to £4.55, you pay with a £10 note and the sales assistant gives you the change. You walk out of the shop with your shopping and discover that the

sales assistant has given you too much change. They've given you change from a £20 note! You look at the change for a bit; and then think – Oh well, that's a bonus! You pocket the extra money and go home. Agree or disagree?

2. *Do you tell your mother?* Your mother gives you £100 and asks you to go to Tottenham Court Road to buy a CD player she's seen advertised for £79.95. You're to take the tube fare from the £100 and the cost of the CD and you can keep the change to buy something for yourself. On your way down the street, you pass another shop with the same CD player – on special offer for £59.95 – and you buy it. When you get home, you tell your mother what a great buy you got and give her the extra £20. Agree or disagree?

3. *What do you say?* You're coming home from school with your friends, and the group of you are talking about everything that's happened today at school. One of your friends asks what you thought about Natalie's news. She had told you that she had an abortion during the school holidays. You hadn't really wanted to think about it; you didn't know what to think. But, now, your friends were all taking sides – she was right; no, she was wrong. Do you agree or disagree?

4. *How do you deal with this situation?* You go into your younger (11-year old) brother or sister's room to borrow something; and you discover some marijuana in their desk. You leave it where it is and say nothing. After all, it's their business. Agree or disagree?

The day continues with lunch, with liturgy preparation and it concludes with Mass.

A service of reconciliation

Here are some notes of a reconciliation service

These notes have been used with a group of candidates preparing to be confirmed. Use it as it is if you think it will work well with your group; but it will be much better if you adapt it to make it your own. I have included one of my own stories about reconciliation. Try to use of one of your stories to make the same point.

The catechists should arrive early to set up the seats in the Church or wherever the service is to take place. Create a 'stage' – a space or a place where the catechists can act out the Gospel and seating around it where the candidates can sit comfortably to see what is happening. There should be a large cross at one end of the 'stage' and the area behind where the candidates are sitting should be darkened if possible. Have some quiet music playing in the background. Give each candidate a stone when they arrive.

A catechist begins session with a prayer and the lighting of the candle.

Welcome by a priest followed by a dialogue between him and catechist A

Priest: There was once a man called Saul. He was a pharisee, a faithful Jew, who believed that the Law, given to his people by God, contained the fullness of the truth – obey the Law to the letter and you would be at rights with God. Break the Law and you get punished.

Catechist A: Now Saul had difficulties with Jesus and those who came after him. The Law said there was only one God. How could Jesus claim to be God's Son, without breaking the Law? Jesus had broken the rules – he was punished by being put to death on the Cross, just as the Law demands.

Priest: When people like Stephen started speaking in Jesus's name, Saul felt that the Law was being flouted all over again. He had a hand in Stephen's killing. As he was stoned to death, for believing in Jesus, the killers put down their coats at Saul's feet. He entirely approved of the killing. After all, if you break the rules, you have to be punished, don't you?

Catechist A: Not long afterwards, Saul made a journey from Jerusalem to Damascus. As he was riding along, a bright light blinded him.

64 Acts 22:7.

He was thrown off his horse and heard the voice of Jesus saying to him, "Saul, Saul, why are you persecuting me?"[64]

Priest: Saul, still blind, hobbled to Damascus, where a holy man called Ananias sought him out and helped him to see again – not with narrow eyes, but with new sight. He began to see with the eyes of faith. He proclaimed his faith in Jesus as the Son of God.

Catechist A: Not long afterwards, Saul changed his name to Paul. From being one of the fiercest persecutors of the Christians, he became their greatest missionary, bringing the good news about Jesus to all the people of the known world, as far as Rome.

Priest: One of the greatest discoveries that Paul made – that God helped him to see – was how harmful the Law had been to him. Instead of setting him free to love God, as it was meant to, it had actually tied him down, made him a slave. He was locked into a cycle; the rules are clear... someone breaks the rules, you punish them. Or do you?

Catechist A: Didn't Jesus change all that? Don't you remember the story of the woman who was caught in the act of adultery? Jesus didn't punish her, did he? In that story, didn't he get the ones who were accusing her to think about what they were doing, to think about the times when they had done things, times when they were not exactly innocent?

The scribes and the Pharisees (the other catechists) arrive with the woman (Catechist B) and present her to Jesus (Catechist C) and the priest tells the story:[65]

Priest The scribes and the Pharisees brought a woman who had been caught in adultery; and making her stand before all of them, they said to him, "Teacher, this woman was caught in the very act of committing adultery. Now in the Law Moses commanded us to stone such women. Now what do you say?" They said this to test him, so that they might have some charge to bring against him.

Catechist C bends down to write in the sand and the priest continues with the story:

Priest Jesus bent down and wrote with his finger on the ground. When they kept on questioning him, he straightened up and said to them, "Let anyone among you who is without sin be the first to throw a stone at her."

Again, Catechist C bends down to write in the sand and the priest continues:

Priest And once again he bent down and wrote on the ground.

---

65 John 8:3-11.

The other catechists (the scribes and Pharisees) freeze holding their stones as if ready to throw them and Catechist A weaves in and out of them looking at each of them and asking a question – as if s/he is their conscience speaking to them:

Catechist A – There are so many ways we bring death and darkness into the world. Being quick to judge people is one of those ways. *Have you judged others unjustly?*

– Our anger and self-righteousness at the offence of another can destroy friendships and relationships. *Have you been angry and self-righteous when someone else has broken the law?*

– We have all broken the law at one time or another and did not get caught. *Have you ever broken the law, and worse still, did you lie to protect yourself?*

– This woman has committed adultery, she has been disloyal to her husband. How selfish! *But wait, have you never been disloyal to your friends; have you never been selfish – concerned only about pleasing yourself?*

– You think this woman has broken the rules and she should be punished. Don't you see that the whole point of the Law is to help us to be free? *Are you so convinced that others should be punished when they do wrong? Are you so unable to forgive?*

Priest When they heard it, they went away, one by one, beginning with the elders; and Jesus was left alone with the woman standing before him.

The other catechists (the scribes and Pharisees) leave, placing their stones at the foot of the cross, moving into the darkened area behind the young people.

Priest Jesus straightened up and said to her, "Woman, where are they? Has no one condemned you?" She said, "No one, sir." And Jesus said, "Neither do I condemn you. Go your way, and from now on do not sin again."

*Catechist C and Catechist B stand up together, Catechist C turns Catechist B around (*metanoia!*) and she moves away.*

The priest and Catechist A move back to the centre and begin to dialogue again.

Catechist A Well, these stories make me think. Here are two stories where people are forgiven. Each of them has hurt other people –
The woman was being disloyal to her husband; imagine how he must have felt! And Paul, he entirely approved of Stephen's killing! He was persecuting the Christians; he believed that you break the Law, you get punished. Simple as that. He couldn't see that God, himself, had broken the rules. In Jesus, God was revealing the true purpose of the Law. Sometimes, we don't see things clearly, huh?

Priest The important thing is, did you notice that both Paul and the woman were forgiven. Paul had to be hit with a bolt of lightening, as it were. Even then, it took him a few days before he was able to see things in a new light. When do you think he was forgiven? And, when do you think he knew he was forgiven? What about the woman? At what point did Jesus forgive her? She knew, of course, that she was forgiven when Jesus told her he didn't condemn her; but when did he really forgive her?

Catechist A You know, that's what it's like with the sacrament of reconciliation, isn't it? I remember the time when I first understood what the sacrament is all about.

My son was about 12 years old. I was working full-time and we had given up having nannies for him. He would stay behind at school to do his homework. He'd get home about 6 o'clock and I wouldn't get home until 6:30 or so. At the time, he just loved ice cream, and each day when he came in from school, he would help himself to some ice cream. Now, we had two different standards of ice cream. We had the usual tubs of ice cream from the supermarket and, being American, we had sauces and whipped cream to dress it up and we also had HäagenDazs ice cream for when we had visitors. Because we had given up having nannies, I was inviting business guests home for dinners and, so, it was important to have something easy but good to give them. Now, my son liked the HäagenDazs ice cream and he was insisting on eating it. I was becoming very impatient about it and I told him that this ice cream belonged to me and that, if he ate it, he was stealing!! One time, when we had some business visitors for dinner, I offered them the HäagenDazs ice cream for desert only to discover that my son had eaten it all – and, what was worse, he had left the empty containers in the freezer. I was just furious!

A couple of weeks later, there was a service of reconciliation in the parish. My son was attending R.E. classes in the parish and his class was asked to come along to the service. My son confessed to the priest that he had stolen my ice cream. To his surprise, the priest asked him when I had forgiven him. My son said he thought I had forgiven him when he had said he was sorry. The priest told him that God had forgiven him as soon as he felt sorry. My son asked the priest why, then, did he have to come to confession. The priest told him that, when we sin, we damage ourselves and we damage our community. It is important that we come together as a community to acknowledge that we fail. We also come together as a community of believers to celebrate the fact that we know that we are never not forgiven.

Priest Let's pause for a moment to think about the times when we have experienced forgiveness; let us think about a time when we have experienced mercy in our lives. [short pause] And, now, let us celebrate that forgiveness in the sacrament of reconciliation [or visit one of the priests for a chat about one of these times and ask for a blessing].
The stone you have been given represents ....

Leave it at the foot of the cross when you ....

We pray as we conclude our service of Reconciliation:

Loving and merciful God,
we thank you for the love of your Son,
who, through his passion, death and resurrection
has freed us from our sins.
Keep us always in your love,
and help us to be faithful followers of your Son,
who lives and reigns, God, forever and ever. Amen.

Blessing and final hymn.

Postscript/Post-Confirmation

A few last comments for the catechists...

After the Confirmation (within a month), meet the newly confirmed young people.

It is very important to ask your newly confirmed young people how they would evaluate their preparation for confirmation. Ask them what was the best thing they experienced; ask if they have any criticisms – anything they think should be changed, impressing on them how important it will be for future candidates.

Ask your young people if they felt well prepared to celebrate the sacrament. Give them the chance to reflect on their experience of the sacramental symbols. This is an important opportunity to help them *own their experience* through a process of reflection. They have been introduced into a fuller and more effective understanding of mysteries through the Gospel message they have learned and, above all, through their experience of the sacrament they have celebrated; and they may have a new perception of their faith, of their Church and of the world.

You might combine this with a celebration. We have found that this is when many of the young people talk about how they can continue to be involved in the parish. Use this as an opportunity to encourage them to continue to do what they have been doing as part of their community projects – or to offer to do other things. Remind them how important they are to the life of our communities. Many young people nowadays ask if they can repeat good experiences they have had of days of recollection or residential retreats – so don't be surprised if some of them ask if they can have a post-Confirmation retreat!

Don't forget to have a catechists' evaluation meeting and celebration too!

Catechists find it very helpful to have an evaluation meeting. Ask:

- what went well – what will you definitely do again
- what didn't go well – and what did you learn from it

Ask, too, if people want to continue to be part of the programme next year. Ask if they feel they need any help or any additional training. And, most importantly, have a celebration to acknowledge the good work you have done and say *thank you* to one another!

And, lastly, a word of acknowledgement and thanks

Over the years, I have worked with so many people in so many parishes – young people, candidates, catechists, parish priests and student priests from the Missionaries of Africa, Comboni and the Consolata missionary societies. It would be impossible to acknowledge every one of them and to thank them individually. I feel very privileged to have had the experience of working with these people and I am very grateful for all I have learned through them. I only hope that, by publishing the programme, others will benefit from all that I have learned. I pray, too, that God will reveal himself to others who use this programme in the way that he has revealed himself to me through it and through all of them.

Diana Klein

Confirmation

Mass of Enrolment

Welcome to all our confirmation candidates, their families and friends. Today, we present you to the parish community.

After the Gospel, The candidates are presented by a catechist, and then they will be asked some questions by the priest. The parents and the parish community are asked if they are willing to support these young people as they prepare to be confirmed.

Catechist 'Father, I am here to present to the parish community the young people of our parish who have asked to join our programme to be prepared for the sacrament of confirmation [and now a list of the candidates is read].' As each person's name is read out, they stand and remain standing.

The priest asks the candidates: 'My young friends, do you want to be enrolled in the programme to be prepared for the sacrament of confirmation?' They reply 'I do' and sit down.

The priest asks their parents: 'Are you willing to support these young people as they prepare for the sacrament of confirmation?' They reply, 'We do.'

The priest asks the parish community: 'Are willing to support and guide the candidates by your prayers and example?' They reply 'We are'.

The priest concludes the presentation by addressing the young people: 'The parish community welcomes you with great joy. You are now enrolled as candidates. May God bless you as you begin your preparations.'

Confirmation

Mass of Commitment

Welcome to all our confirmation candidates, their families and friends. Today, our young people are committing themselves to continue in the parish programme for preparation for the sacrament of confirmation.

Catechist 'Bishop N... will be celebrating the Sacrament of confirmation here in our parish on [date]. I would like to present to the parish our young people who are preparing to celebrate the sacrament. [A list of the candidates is now read]. As each person's name is read out, they stand and remain standing.
When all the names have been called out, the priest will ask them to sit.

The priest asks the catechist: 'in the name of this community, you and the other catechists have been working to prepare these young people for the sacrament of confirmation. 'Do they understand the importance of what they are doing?' The catechist replies, 'They do'.
The priest asks, 'Are they willing to continue to take part conscientiously in the preparation programme?' The catechist replies, 'They are'.

The priest then addresses the candidates saying 'Do you agree to take part in the sessions and activities that are a part of this programme? Are you willing to open your minds and hearts to the activities of the Holy Spirit during this time of preparation? And, do you pray for a deeper growth in faith and hope and love?' They reply, 'We do'.

C2

The priest asks the parents of the candidates and the parish community if they are willing to continue to support and pray for these young people as they continue to prepare for the sacrament of confirmation and they reply, 'We are'.

The priest concludes by addressing the young people: 'May God bless you as you continue your preparations for the sacrament of confirmation.'

C3